Empiricism and its evolution

Empiricism
and its evolution
A Marxist View

George Novack

PATHFINDER
NEW YORK LONDON MONTREAL SYDNEY

ISBN 978-0-87348-020-8
Library of Congress Catalog Card Number 68-59426
Manufactured in Canada

First edition, 1969
Sixteenth printing, 2025

COVER PAINTING: Herman Heyenbrock, *Steelworks*, pastel, ca. 1919.

Pathfinder
pathfinderpress.com
Email: pathfinder@pathfinderpress.com

To the veterans of
American Trotskyism who
never succumbed to empiricism or
impressionism but steadfastly adhered to
dialectical materialism and its
revolutionary perspectives—and to the
younger leaders who have learned from
them and will go beyond them.

CONTENTS

FOREWORD

Most works on philosophy nowadays, apart from popularizations for the general public, are written by professors for other academic specialists to read. That is not the purpose of this book. It is primarily addressed to students who have encountered references to empiricism and want to know what that mode of thought is all about.

These chapters aim to answer the following questions:

What did empiricism teach? How did empiricist philosophy develop? What role has empiricism played in Western thought and what did it accomplish? What distinguishes the modern empiricist, *i.e.*, what habits of thought nurture and are nurtured by empiricism? What attitude does dialectical materialism take toward this kind of philosophy?

The term "empiricism" has a twofold meaning. It refers both to a specific type of philosophizing which occupies a particular place in the history of modern thought and to certain customary ways of thinking which are taken as "common sense." These two aspects of intellectual activity coexist in close relation and reinforce each other.

Empirical habits of mind have preceded the philosophy of empiricism and will outlive it. They arise spontaneously out of the first superficial and uncritical experiences of everyday life. These elementary procedures and simplified results of commonsense thinking form the base and beginning of all understanding of the world around us. As the primary and provisional phases of knowledge, they cannot be avoided or dispensed with. They are especially useful in providing a preliminary orientation in theory or practice amidst novel circumstances or surroundings.

But these first impressions and unreliable inductions can be surpassed and improved upon. They mark the initiation, not the completion, of scientific thought.

The original empirical school owed a large measure of its effectiveness to its recognition of the truth that all knowledge depends on sense experience of the external world. This central principle of its theory of knowledge explained the source and power of ideas as satisfactorily as the scientific data of its heyday permitted.

Some earlier philosophers had taught that human knowledge must be based on sense experience. Among the Greeks, thinkers who were otherwise so unlike as Democritus and Aristotle assigned the primary role in the process of knowledge to sense experience. Even such eminent schoolmen as Thomas Aquinas and Albert the Great aspired to develop their science of nature through a rational interpretation of sense experience rather than on Christian revelation.

However, except for the Atomists, these ancient and medieval schools did not make the origin of knowledge in sense experience the governing principle which was central to their whole system of thought. That was the epoch-making innovation of Locke and his successors.

Empiricism participated in the promotion of philosophy and science under the impetus of the bourgeois transformation of Western society. By refuting the obsolete categories of scholastic thought, which had gained dominance under European feudalism, in favor of the new scientific ideas and methods, empiricism equipped philosophy with keener insight into reality and with more fruitful instruments of knowledge. By demonstrating that all our ideas come from experience through sensation and are then refined by reflection, and by extending this principle of explanation to many fields of knowledge, classical empiricism made enduring contributions to human understanding.

Every subsequent school of philosophy has had to come to terms with this theory of knowledge and its findings. Just as capitalism created the economic preconditions and social forces for its own supersession by a higher mode of production, so the empirical expression of its world outlook elaborated some of the key ideas required for a fully scientific method of thought.

However, it was no more the last word in philosophy than purely empirical procedures are the sole and perfected techniques of scientific method. Empirical methods in science—the collection, observation, and comparison of data; experimentation wherever objects can be influenced and changed by technological means; counting and measuring; search for regularities within the particulars of experience—all remain as enduring achievements.

But these indispensable acquisitions of human knowledge and its means of discovery are not identical with the *philosophy* of empiricism. From Locke to the present, this philosophy has been based on certain mechanical conceptions or metaphysical assumptions which have turned out to be incorrect. It thus yields inadequate means of analyzing and explaining reality.

The cumulative effects of the changes in social relations and the advances in science and philosophy over the past two centuries have served to expose the limitations of the purely empirical outlook, while it has more and more been transformed from a high-powered accelerator of intellectual activity into a brake on further theoretical progress. In philosophy the premises and positions of British empiricism were outstripped on one side by the eighteenth-century French school of materialism and on the other by German thinkers from Kant through Hegel to Feuerbach. Its doctrines became definitively anachronistic with the creation of dialectical materialism in the mid-nineteenth century.

This fact has yet to be recognized by most thinkers in the English-speaking world. They are still enthralled by empiricism and would hotly dispute the assertion that its usefulness has been exhausted. The opinion persists on both sides of the Atlantic that an empirically oriented philosophy, properly amended and brought up to date, remains the best approach to the manifold problems of nature, society, and science.

It is a gauge of the provincialism of English thought that its current representatives, from professors to labor leaders, cling to empirical assumptions long after their inconsistencies, inadequacies, and errors have been disclosed. It is no less a sign of the retarded state of theory in the United States that the most popular schools of philosophy, pragmatism and the varieties of positivism, adhere tenaciously to the basic conceptions of empiricism after these have been superseded by the achievements of thought elsewhere.

This book aims to trace the evolution, filiations, and outcome of the empirical school from its origins in seventeenth-century England to some of its contemporary manifestations in theory and practice. It will investigate the source of its strength and successes along with the reasons for its failings and enfeeblement. This survey should clarify the necessity for the replacement of empiricism by a more correct and comprehensive philosophy—dialectical materialism, which has assimilated the truths taught by empiricism but overcome the inherent defects of its central tenets.

Several chapters of this book were originally written for British readers; two appeared in the London socialist publication, *Labour Review,* in 1958. That accounts for the slant of the arguments and the choice of illustrations in those parts of this exposition which are directed to the empirical habits of thought embedded in the British labor and socialist movements.

Nonetheless, the same arguments are fully pertinent to the United States. Our culture suffers from as great a backwardness in theoretical matters as exists in Great Britain, whence the empirical philosophy, like so much else in the American past, was imported. The United States long ago attained political and economic independence from its mother country; it has yet to cast off its philosophical dependence.

A long line of thinkers from Emerson to John Dewey attempted to devise a national philosophy corresponding to the special conditions, needs, and perspectives of the American people. They did eventually succeed in creating pragmatism. However, this homegrown ideology is, with all its modifications, essentially a New World version of empiricism, as the next to the last chapter seeks to demonstrate.

A quite different type of thought is now required to move beyond the limitations of empiricism in all its guises and arrive at a world-view suited to the intellectual and practical demands of our revolutionary era of transition from capitalism to socialism. The name of that philosophy is dialectical materialism; it provides the instruments of analysis which have, in this work, been applied to a criticism of the empirical tradition.

George Novack
February 1, 1968

1

The beginnings of empiricism

Since the seventeenth century, empiricism, in one form or another, has been the major philosophy of the English speaking peoples on both sides of the Atlantic. The long dominance of this type of thought coincides with the period of bourgeois rule in Britain and its extension to other parts of the world. Britain has one of the oldest capitalist cultures, and empiricism is a characteristic product of that culture.

Empiricism and capitalist culture

The connection between the philosophical method of empiricism and the social system of capitalism is not an accidental but an organic one. In its theoretical content, empiricism is a view of the world. It performs a definite social function as a method of thinking appropriate to specific historical conditions and by serving the class requirements of the bourgeoisie. The periods of the birth, maturity, and senescence of empiricism are bound up with the rise and decay of the bourgeois mode of existence.

Empiricism in its youth was an integral part of the mightiest technological, economic, political, scientific, artistic, and philosophical revolution England has yet experienced. This many-sided transformation of Britain arose from the commercial and industrial advances and advantages which enabled the British bourgeoisie to build up the capitalist economy and establish its political rule in the seventeenth century.

Empiricism was born as bourgeois society's philosophical challenge to the scholastic, Roman Catholic ideological superstructure of feudalism. The religious aspect of this process began with Wycliffe and Lollardry, continued through the Reformation of the English Church and its break with Rome, and culminated in Puritanism. Empiricism drew many of its key ideas from the world outlook stimulated by the new phase in the natural sciences and identified with such figures as Copernicus, Kepler, Galileo, Huyghens, Descartes, Gassendi, Boyle, Harvey, and Newton.

Empiricism was not the most revolutionary theoretical product of this period. A substantial school of materialists held the advanced outposts. Yet, in its boldest forms, empiricism bordered on materialist positions and was originally an extremely radical departure in the field of philosophy.

Classical British empiricism proved to be an invaluable theoretical tool in the tasks of destruction and renovation undertaken by the bourgeois-democratic forces of the seventeenth and eighteenth centuries. From Bacon to Hume, it acted as a powerful stimulant to progress in Western thought. It challenged medieval ideas, shattered scholasticism, dislodged many props of feudal theology, and undercut established modes of idealism. It sought to devise a new logic and a more fruitful method of investigation of natural phenomena, of society, and of the reasoning processes to replace the formalized logic and sterile speculations of the scholastics. It aided the revival of materialism and helped clear the ground for the growth of the natural and social sciences.

Empiricism thus earned a lasting place in the historical development of modern thought. Its successes have been so great and the influence of its methods and ideas so widespread and enduring that they have entered into the very bloodstream of Anglo-American culture, until now they appear to many people as the normal, natural, eternal attributes of human reasoning.

Bacon: the inspirer of empiricism

All the power and promise inherent in empiricism was contained in the writings of Sir Francis Bacon (1561–1626), that illustrious innovator of modern philosophy. Bacon may be regarded as the father of British materialism and the grandfather of empiricism.

Bacon set British philosophy on a new road in the following ways:

1) By a very backhanded concession to theology he severed natural philosophy from religion. He did so by maintaining that humans could not know God's nature by means of reason or sensation but only through revelation of His inspired word. By being separated from theology, natural science was allocated a definite territory of its own in which it could expand more freely. Unintentionally, but none the less effectively for that, Bacon initiated a process of differentiating philosophy and science from theology which, when carried forward by later thinkers, undermined the theological foundations of religious dogmas and so cleared a path

for materialist and even directly atheist conclusions.

2) By divorcing philosophy from theology and reason from faith, Bacon joined the new philosophy to natural science in the form of a materialist physics. He directed men's attention away from the barren scholastic learning of the universities* towards outdoor study and direct observation of natural phenomena.

3) Bacon proceeded from a materialist conception of nature which viewed matter as indestructible, self-moving, ever active, and constantly changing. Although God had created nature, he did not interfere with its causal order.

4) Bacon based his philosophy not upon metaphysics (*i.e.*, upon learned disputes about the meanings of terms or unverifiable abstractions) but upon methodical investigation of the "universal process of motion" (*i.e.*, upon physics, especially mechanics).

5) Bacon projected a new logical method. This relied not upon what he called the "vicious habit" of jumping to unverified general propositions and deducing consequences from them, but rather upon the procedure of making narrow general propositions from observed data and then, step by step, moving from these restricted rules to broader generalizations and checking them at every stage by reference to the results of experiment.

6) This empirical and inductive method, depending upon the observation of nature, inquiry, and experiment rather than upon abstract propositions, stressed work-

---

* The method of developing men's knowledge of the world adopted by the scholastic philosophy was to take a general proposition of, usually, Aristotle, and reconstruct an account of the world by purely deductive methods—*i.e.*, by deducing what the world "must" be like on the unquestioned and unquestionable assumption that Aristotle's general proposition was *absolutely* correct. There are, of course, modern scholastics and they are to be found not only in theological seminaries.

ability instead of formal consistency as the test of truth. "What is most useful in practice is most correct in theory," Bacon wrote. "For truth is shown and proved by the evidence of works. . . ."

7) Bacon switched the main function of philosophy from providing theoretical arguments for religious dogmas to serving the practical needs of mankind. The increased knowledge of nature acquired through Bacon's innovations in scientific method was intended to promote useful works and to stimulate inventions like printing, gunpowder, and the magnetic compass. Such mechanical advances increased the efficiency and power of the instruments of production, augmented wealth, and helped satisfy men's needs and comforts more fully. Bacon declared his aim when he wrote that he was seeking "the knowledge of Causes, and Secret Motions of Things; and the Enlarging of the bounds of Humane Empire to the effecting of all things possible."

These aims corresponded to basic requirements of the emerging bourgeois order. Bacon sought to devise "an engine" of thought adequate for the social practices of the new era. His theorizing heralded the coming industrial revolution. He announced that wedding of natural science and industry which has showered so many benefits upon mankind.

For Bacon, experience, based upon what we learn through the senses and aids to the senses like the telescope, was the sole valid source and sure road to useful knowledge. Unlike most of his empirical successors, he did not interpret sensuous experience as primarily passive. He was one of the first to emphasize that the acquisition of knowledge had its active side in the manipulating and shaping of objects as is done by a craftsman. It is through such practical activity that the senses disclose the essential features of nature to us.

These tendencies in his thought bore fruit in various ways in the seventeenth century. During the English Civil War, the materialism he pioneered acquired an aristocratic and monarchist form in the hands of his companion Thomas Hobbes (1588–1679) and a plebeian and democratic expression in the Leveller leader, Richard Overton (1597–1663).

The classical empiricism of Locke

The purely empirical aspect of Bacon's thought was developed later in the century and under different circumstances by John Locke.

John Locke (1632–1704) was the founder of the empirical school of philosophy. The empiricists did not have to produce any comprehensive cosmological theory of their own. They simply took over, ready made, the mechanical conception of the world from the natural scientists of the seventeenth century. They aimed to create a theory of knowledge in line with the premises of natural science and to extend the methods of thought which were achieving such brilliant results in the natural sciences to the problems of philosophy and the study of mankind.

Empiricism is based not so much upon a particular view of the world as upon a statement concerning the ways and means of acquiring knowledge of the world. It is in fact a special theory of knowledge—an epistemological theory. *The primary principle of empiricism is that all knowledge is founded on experience of the senses.*

Hobbes stated that sensation was "the principle of the knowledge of principles" themselves and all science is derived from that source. He wrote in *Leviathan:* ". . . there is no conception in a man's mind which hath not at first, totally or by parts, been begotten upon the organs of sense. The rest are derived from that original."

Locke approached the problem of the origins and basis of knowledge along the same line. He wrote:

> Let us suppose the mind to be, as we say, white paper, void of all characters, without any ideas; how comes it to be furnished? . . . To this I answer in one word, from experience: in that all our knowledge is founded, and from that it ultimately derives itself.

This proposition was directed against the idealist theory, propounded in Locke's time by, among others, the Cambridge Platonists, that knowledge is somehow drawn from innate notions implanted in the mind before birth and deriving ultimately from God, their author. Thus, in 1660, in a discourse called *Of the Immortality of the Soul,* one of the Cambridge Platonists, John Smith, spoke about

> The Archetypall Ideas of Justice, Wisdome, Goodness, Truth, Eternity, Omnipotency, and all these either Morall, Physicall or Metaphysical notions, which are either the First Principles of Science or the ultimate complement and final perfection of it. These we always find to be the same and know that no Exorcisms of material mutation have any power over them; though we ourselves are but of yesterday and mutable every moment; yet these are Eternall and depend not upon any mundane vicissitudes; neither could we ever gather them from our observation of any Material thing where they were never sown.

Referring to such "Eternall Archetypall Ideas," Locke remarked:

> It is an established opinion among some men that there are in the understanding certain innate principles, some

> primary notions, characters, as it were, stamped upon the mind of man, which the soul receives in its very first being and brings into the world with it.

Locke set out to demolish this supposition of the Platonists, but, as we shall see, only partly succeeded in this task.

The original source of ideas

Locke relies on plain empirical evidence, or rather the absence of it, to disprove the existence of innate ideas. If there were self-evident truths, he argued, these should be present in all men and clear to savages, infants, and even idiots. In fact, this is not so; the supposed innate principles in religion, logic, morals, and mathematics are consciously held only by educated minds.

This theory of empiricism is true so far as it goes. However, it cannot be said to provide a complete theory of knowledge. Whatever ideas or knowledge we do have ultimately derive from physical contacts with the world around us, through our senses.

This is denied by proponents of the idealist school who teach that some, if not all, of our ideas come from an immaterial source. They have used this doctrine to uphold the existence of eternal and self-evident truths in religion, morals, and logic. Ever since this view was expressed in classical Greece by such philosophers as Pythagoras, Socrates, and Plato, the idealists have held up mathematics as the surest evidence that general ideas could not possibly be taken from sense experience. Berkeley tells us: "Number is no object of sense: it is an act of the mind."

Dr. Whewell, an English historian of science of the early nineteenth century, maintained, following Plato, that such propositions as two and three make five are "necessary truths," *i.e.*, truths which have a certainty, universality, and stability mere experience could not give. John Stuart Mill replied that this simple arithmetical statement expresses "a truth known to us by early and constant experience . . . which rests on the evidence of sense."

The empiricist Mill was right on this point against the Kantian idealist Whewell. The "early and constant experience," out of which simple arithmetic emerged and on which it is based, belongs not only to childhood but to the childhood of mankind. The art of counting originated among the savages through their handling and observation of definite objects for specific social purposes. If there were no such objects in men's ordinary experience of the world they live in, there would be no need or use for the science of enumeration. Numbers are still taught to children by pointing to their fingers and toes, beads, blocks, and so on—that is to say, through the evidence provided by their organs and senses of touch and sight.

There are some primitives who cannot count beyond ten and have no special words in their language for numbers greater than five. Our own decimal numeration testifies to its lowly origins and bodily basis, since we reckon by tens in accord with the primitive practice of depending upon fingers and toes for calculation. Today, in the construction of electronic computers, mathematicians find the binary system, *i.e.*, a system using a base of two instead of ten numbers, to be most suitable.

Similarly, other mathematical concepts and methods may be traced back to their sensory and social roots. Thus the very example of number which the idealists bring forward to prove the immaterial sources of ideas may be used to show the truth of the empirical assertion of their earthly origins.

The persistence of the belief in the immaterial origin of mathematics is demonstrated by the fact that Hume, the otherwise ruthlessly consistent sensationalist, puts mathematical propositions, including arithmetic, into a different class from ideas about matters of fact. He assigns them to a category of purely abstract "Relations of Ideas" which are "without dependence on what is anywhere existent in the Universe."

The ambiguities of empiricism

We stated at the outset that empiricism is first of all a theory of *knowledge* (epistemology), not a theory of *being* (ontology). Locke's classical exposition of empiricism is aptly called *An Essay Concerning Human Understanding.* Locke says that he will not venture on "the vast ocean of being"—although he cannot help diving into it now and then.

The conscious limitation of empiricist thought to epistemology alone was the source of its most serious weakness. Empiricism came into the world with an ineradicable birthmark—an inherent ambiguity. The empiricist proceeds from the premise that all knowledge is based on experience. But he is not clear on two further questions: (a) what generates this experience? and (b) what are the things which experience informs us about?

Materialism, unlike empiricism, gives a plain and direct answer to these two questions. It states that objective, physical being precedes animal and human sensation, perception, and knowledge. It insists that all the "furniture" in man's mind comes from his interactions and connections with the social and natural environments. Materialism insists upon the *unity* of objective being and subjective thought.

Empiricism as such, however, does not commit itself wholeheartedly on these crucial points. Locke defined knowledge as "nothing but the perception of the connection and agreement or disagreement and repugnancy of any of our ideas." This definition can be interpreted in two opposing ways. If this "agreement" of which Locke speaks is taken to consist in the correspondence of ideas with their objects in the external world, that coincides with the materialist view. John Toland (1670–1722), a blunt and therefore embarrassing materialist disciple of Locke, drove this point home when he defined the basic principle of evidence in his philosophy as "the exact conformity of our Ideas or Thoughts with their Objects, or the Things we think upon."

If, however, this agreement is regarded merely as the harmony of ideas with one another, or with sense-data which are self-enclosed and have no essential bonds with material reality, the door is left open for idealist conclusions.

Thus an inconsistency, an inconclusiveness, even a certain shiftiness is implanted in the very heart of the empirical philosophy. This makes it possible for empiricists to swing in either direction on this pivotal question of the relation between thought and being. That is also why empiricism by its very nature is a theory of knowledge particularly suited to individuals and social groupings, like the middle classes in bourgeois society, who are themselves inconsistent, unstable, caught between contending forces and unwilling to commit themselves decisively on decisive matters.

Here is another instance of the same sort of ambiguity in Locke. He asked whether, when we have ideas in our minds "we can thence certainly infer the existence of anything without us which corresponds to that idea . . . whereof some men think there may be a question made." Locke repudiated this suggestion implied in the question of the skeptics. He states in reply that there is a manifest difference between dreaming of being in a fire and actually being in it, and that in practical life we are certain of this difference and guide ourselves by it. Our knowledge is accurate and real, Locke teaches, and there is "a conformity between our ideas and the reality of things."

This is good materialist doctrine. At the same time, however, Locke holds that the knowledge derived from sensation is inferior in certainty and clarity to that knowledge which is presumably obtained through the superior channels of demonstration and intuition. According to him, we are intuitively aware of what spirit, the soul, and God are, but have no clear idea of material substance. The latter "is merely the something, we know not what . . . the supposed, but unknown support of those qualities we find existing." This "we know not what" is the seed out of which Kant's theory of the unknowable thing-in-itself grew and nineteenth-century agnosticism ("we know not if") emerged.

The social source of Locke's inconsistencies

Locke's writings are filled with such inconsistencies, which are lamented by many critics as the source of confusion in his thought and weakness in his philosophical structure. His critics are correct here, but these self-same commentators fail to grasp the historical source and the *class necessity* of this evasiveness. Locke's theory, with its inconsistencies, most effectively served the English bourgeoisie. What was weakness from the viewpoint of formal symmetry of doctrine was strength in the service of rising capitalism.

Basil Willey has well observed: "Locke's theory of knowledge reveals that quality which his philosophy shares with the Church of England and perhaps other English things, its power to comprehend in a vague synthesis principles really belonging to opposite schools of thought." (*The Seventeenth-Century Background,* pp. 274–5) This "English" quality is basically bourgeois in origin. It is equally prominent in the governmental organization of England which crowned the seventeenth-century bourgeois revolutions. What an incongruous yet ingenious combination of institutions, derived from different ages, this state structure was—and so remains to this very day. The Monarchy, the Established Church, and a House of Lords, all carried over from feudalism and every one subordinated to the sovereignty of the House of Commons, parliamentarism!

Locke's thought exhibits similar mixtures of contraries. These constitute the distinctive quality of his philosophy. It must be remembered that he was the principal ideologist of the *victorious* bourgeois revolution in England—a revolution which ended in a compromise between the bourgeoisie and the aristocracy and which sought to consolidate its positions rather than move forward to higher ground. Locke as an ideologist was called upon to *reconcile* the conflicting claims of Christianity and practical philosophy, of divine revelation and bourgeois reason, of the existence of a State Church with the toleration of the prime institution of bourgeois nonconformist sects, of the King with Parliament, of traditional beliefs with new discoveries and progressive ideas, of the rights of men with the demands of private property. It would have been impossible to satisfy both sides fully and maintain consistency.

Locke, for example, is regarded as the architect of religious tolerance in England. Yet he refused to grant freedom of worship and thought either to Catholics or atheists because these extremes were repugnant to the new bourgeois regime.

Locke did not hesitate to sacrifice theoretical consistency for the sake of arriving at practical compromises and ideological combinations that gained his ends! He believed that principles should not be the master but the servant of practical necessity. Is not the English crown Presbyterian in Scotland and Episcopal in England? This was the very spirit of the British bourgeoisie of Locke's epoch, and of even later periods of British history. No wonder that Locke became the favorite philosopher of conciliators and compromisers, the patron saint of liberalism, the apostle of "the middle way."

Thus the dualisms inherent in empiricism derive historically from the difficult position of the British bourgeoisie, who fought against the feudalists on one side and were hard pressed by the plebeians on the other. The needs of the struggle against the old order gave a radical sharpness to empiricism (and even a revolutionary impulse to its later influence in America and France), while fear of the lower classes blunted the edge of its criticism and restrained its representatives from going all the way in their theoretical expressions and practical conclusions.

Subsequently this very indefiniteness of empirical philosophy appealed to thinkers, especially those connected with the petty bourgeoisie, who were caught in similar social contradictions. The empiricists are the philosophical incarnation of Bunyan's character "Mr. Facing-Both-Ways"—a character quite common in Britain and in the United States today.

2

British empiricism and natural science

The peculiar traits of British empiricism, and especially its pronounced dualities, cannot be explained without examining its affinities with the natural science of the seventeenth century.

Classical empiricism and mechanical science

The empirical and mechanical trends in natural science, initiated in England by Gilbert (1544–1603) and Harvey (1578–1657) and more fully cultivated by Hooke (1635–1703), Boyle (1627–1691), Newton (1642–1727), and other members of the Royal Society, exerted direct and powerful influence upon the formation of empirical philosophy. Locke, a friend of Boyle and Newton, regarded his theory of knowledge as a philosophical counterpart to the work of these master-builders of natural science.

Mechanics was the central science of Locke's time; the conceptions derived from that branch of natural science dominated the philosophizing of the age. Mechanics took this commanding position because the most vital concerns of bourgeois society were tied up with the requirements of water transport, mining and metallurgy, and military engineering. These decisive branches of social-economic activity put the major technical and theoretical problems before the scientific investigators of the early capitalist epoch.

Their inquiries concentrated on the analysis of the displacement of physical masses in space and time. From their researches in physics and astronomy, these pioneer scientists arrived at a particular mechanical-mathematical conception of nature, which was sketched out by Descartes (1596–1650) and filled in by the atomism of his philosophical opponent, the materialist Pierre Gassendi (1592–1655).

According to this conception, the world consisted of matter in motion. Matter was divided into tiny particles (corpuscles, atoms) and was essentially inert. Motion was impressed upon bodies by some external force and was exclusively local in character. The different bodies in nature and their diverse properties were generated by variations in the local motions of material substances striking against one another. "I look upon the phenomena of nature to be caused by the local motion of one part of matter hitting against another," wrote Boyle.

Neither magnetism, discovered by Hooke, nor gravitation, investigated by Newton, fitted into this mechanical scheme since they appeared to depend upon action at a distance. But these anomalous modes of motion were left to shift for themselves. The simple mechanical action of large and small masses impinging from without upon one another was conceived as the fundamental form of material motion.

Despite the central role played by gravitation, Newton gave a tremendous boost to the mechanical view of nature when he united celestial with terrestrial mechanics. His universal laws of motion sought to explain all material movements from the orbits of the whirling planets to the fall of a stone on earth. These movements were analyzed in mechanical terms, quantitatively expressed in mathematical formulas.

The various schools of bourgeois philosophy in England prepared, promoted, and shared this mechanical outlook. The materialists, Bacon and Hobbes, most consistently formulated these theoretical tendencies of natural science. Bacon remarked that "nature knows only mechanical causation, by the investigation of which all our efforts should be directed." Hobbes went much further. He tried to squeeze all types of movement, from the operations of nature to social and political actions and the processes of the human mind, into the framework of purely mechanical categories.

The empiricists did not draw such sweeping conclusions from the premises of the mechanical doctrine as the materialists, but they proceeded, up to a point, along parallel lines. Locke accepted the mechanical view of nature as the foundation of his theory of knowledge. This entangled him in a knot of theoretical difficulties.

The limitations of human knowledge

The first problem the mechanical philosophy presented to Locke was whether true knowledge of the material world was possible, and how much of it was available to mankind. It was certainly paradoxical that the capacities of the human mind should have become questioned at a time when men were expanding their positive knowledge of the world at an unprecedented rate. But the theoretical dilemmas arising from these very advances of the natural sciences and the new mechanical world-view were among the compelling reasons why Locke undertook his inquiry into the origins, nature, and extent of human knowledge.

Boyle and Newton doubted whether the natural reason of man, shut up in a small portion of the brain, could attain true knowledge of the inner nature of things. Newton, for example, ascribed no cause to gravitation; he was content to accept this cosmic force as a given fact. Thus the most fundamental force then known remained an unexplained property of matter, the effect of some unknown cause.

Newton had sound scientific reasons for refusing to speculate on the cause of gravitation. Gravitation is observed as a property of huge aggregations of matter: the earth, the sun, and other celestial bodies. The effects of gravitation could be observed, described, and formulated; but, because of their colossal scale, could not readily be harnessed, experimented with, or produced by laboratory means.

Chemistry, not to speak of other sciences, was still in its infancy, as were capitalist industry and its experimental techniques. Natural processes for the most part could be observed but not reproduced in laboratories. Under such conditions it appeared plausible that no more could be known about things than certain of their outward manifestations, while their innermost essence must remain inaccessible. What was still unreachable, unproducible, and unreproducible in the social and technological practice of the period appeared forever incomprehensible to the empirical theory of knowledge.

How Locke's theory of knowledge reflected the immature development of science is graphically shown in the following quotations:

> Another great cause of ignorance is the want of ideas we are capable of . . . Bulk, figure, and motion, we have

ideas of. But though we are not without ideas of these primary qualities of bodies in general, yet not knowing what is the particular bulk, figure, and motion, of the greatest part of the bodies of the universe, we are ignorant of the several powers, efficacies, and ways of operation, whereby the effects which we daily see are produced. These are hid from us, in some things by being too remote; and, in others, by being too minute. When we consider the vast distance of the known and visible parts of the world, and the reasons we have to think that what lies within our ken is but a small part of the universe, we shall then discover a huge abyss of ignorance. What are the particular fabrics of the great masses of matter which make up the whole stupendous frame of corporeal beings; how far they are extended; what is their motion, and how continued or communicated; and what influence they have one upon another, are contemplations that at first glimpse, our thoughts lose themselves in. If we narrow our contemplations, and confine our thoughts to this little canton—I mean this system of our sun, and the grosser masses of matter that visibly move about it, what several sorts of vegetables, animals and intellectual corporeal beings, infinitely different from those of our little spot of earth, may there probably be in the other planets, to the knowledge of which, even of their outward figures and parts, we can no way attain whilst we are confined to this earth; there being no natural means, either by sensation or reflection, to convey their certain ideas into our minds? They are out of reach of those inlets of all our knowledge; and what sorts of furniture and inhabitants those mansions contain in them, we cannot so much as guess, much less have clear and distinct ideas of them. (*An Essay Concerning Human Understanding,* Book IV, p. 452)

Locke's pessimism over the possibility of ever attaining scientific knowledge of the universe or even the planetary system was a concomitant of the technological backwardness of his society. Astronomical photography, spectrum analysis, and radioscopy were music of the future.

His pessimism extended equally to the atomic world:

> If a great, nay far the greatest part of the several ranks of bodies in the universe escape our notice by their remoteness, there are others that are no less concealed from us by their minuteness. These *insensible corpuscles* being the active parts of matter, and the great instruments of nature, on which depend not only all their secondary qualities, but also most of their natural operations, our want of precise distinct ideas of their primary qualities keeps us in an incurable ignorance of what we desire to know about them. I doubt not but if we would discover the figure, size, texture, and motion of the minute constituent parts of any two bodies, we should know without trial several of their operations one upon another, as we do now the properties of a square or a triangle. Did we know the mechanical affections of the particles of rhubarb, hemlock, opium, and a man, as a watchmaker does those of a watch, whereby it performs its operations; and of a file, which by rubbing on them will alter the figure of any of the wheels; we should be able to tell beforehand that rhubarb will purge, hemlock kill, and opium make a man sleep; as well as a watchmaker can, that a little piece of paper laid on the balance will keep the watch from going till it be removed; or that some small part of it being rubbed by a file, the machine would quite lose its motion, and the watch go no more. The dissolving of silver in aqua fortis, and gold in aqua regia, and not vice versa, would be then perhaps no more difficult to know, than it is to a smith to understand

> why the turning of one key will open a lock, and not the turning of another. But whilst we are destitute of sense acute enough to discover the minute particles of bodies, and to give us ideas of their mechanical affections, we must be content to be ignorant of their properties and ways of operation; nor can we be assured about them any farther than some few trials we make are able to reach. But whether they will succeed again another time, we cannot be certain. This hinders our certain knowledge of universal truths concerning natural bodies; and our reason carries us herein very little beyond particular matter of fact. (*Ibid.*, pp. 452–3)

We may imagine Locke's surprise, and possibly the adjustments he would have made in his theory of knowledge, could he have witnessed, two centuries later, Mendeleyev's successful predictions of both the physical and chemical properties of three elements mankind had not yet discovered. But in Locke's time the "clearest and most enlarged understandings of thinking men find themselves puzzled and at a loss in every particle of matter."

Accepting the transitory limitations upon scientific development at that given state as forever fixed and insuperable, the empiricists made them into the cornerstone of their theory of knowledge (or rather, of the limitations upon knowledge). They treated effects as though they gave no clues to the character of their causes and could be considered independently of them. They regarded summaries of observable facts as adequate explanations for phenomena. In such a view it became unnecessary to get at the causal origins and essential constitution of the forces of nature; it was enough to trace out the coordination of their manifestations.

This habit of thought subsequently, in the nineteenth

century, became a cardinal doctrine of a new school of empiricism called positivism. Positivism substituted ordered descriptions of the observed sequences of phenomena for the discovery of their inner causes and organic connections.

Locke shared the belief of Boyle and Newton that the intrinsic nature of material reality is cut off from direct human observations and thereby shut off from human knowledge. He pictured the world as composed of independent, self-determining, unchangeable substances. But then he stated that the mind of men could not penetrate to the "real constitution" of substance. We cannot form any idea of "the secret abstract nature of substance in general," he said; it was a supposed "we know not what."

The presumed unknowability of substance played a key role in Locke's theory; his doctrine of the inescapable imperfections of our knowledge is based upon it. "We may be convinced," he wrote, "that the ideas we attain to by our faculties are very disproportionate to things themselves, when a positive, clear distinct one of substance itself, which is the foundation of all the rest, is concealed from us." If we cannot have any idea of substance, then it is equally impossible, concluded Locke, for us to know the real constitution of the two great divisions of substance: bodies, which are material substances, or minds, which are spiritual substances.

Locke's theory of substance contains the germ of the skepticism and subjectivism which were lodged like a latent infection within empiricism and ultimately ravaged it. The theoretical source of his error lay in his absolute separation of material substantiality from the qualities of things. Locke could not find any substance in the world, or any clear idea of it in his mind, because he totally detached the "substratum" of things from the qualities they exhibited.

However, substance does not have any concrete existence or determinate content apart from its qualities; without these it is nothing but an empty abstraction. Fruit does not exist except in specific material forms of apples, pears, peaches, etc. Locke's quest for "a pure substance" in general, which is "the same everywhere," was bound to be as vain and illusory as the search for fruit without the definite characteristics of members of that species.

Locke's difficulties did not end with the contradictory conception of substances which existed, but whose real constitution was inaccessible and inscrutable. The mechanical doctrine landed Locke into similar difficulties in respect to the qualities of things as a reliable source of knowledge about the world around us. Like Galileo, Descartes, Boyle, and Newton, Locke divided qualities into two opposing groups: primary ones like "solidity, extension, motion and rest and number" and secondary ones like colors, smells, tastes, sounds.

The first actually inhered in bodies; they were objective and permanent aspects of things which provided the basis for a dependable knowledge of nature. The secondary qualities were the effects of the powers of the primary ones upon ourselves. They were subjective, fluctuating, confusing ideas which hung like a deceitful shimmering curtain between our minds and the external world.

Locke did not have valid *empirical* grounds for dividing qualities into two such opposing groups—properties of things and contents of sensation—one with objective existence and the other essentially subjective. Taken strictly from the standpoint of sensory experience, which is the supreme standard for empiricism, both kinds of qualities stood upon the same level. Solidity, for example, which Locke classified as a primary quality, is an aspect of things which depends as much upon the impression of the senses as do color and sound, which he regarded as secondary and subjective. The solidity of metals is relative; under certain conditions their constitution is porous and penetrable. X-rays will pass through so solid an object as a crystal, showing in the process its lattice structure.

Locke was impelled to draw so sharp a distinction between the two types of qualities, not for empirical reasons, but because the mechanical system, which was the model of scientific knowledge for him, demanded it. Mechanics had singled out these particular features of the world for special status, not because they were primary in sense experience, but rather because they were foremost in the solution of the problems of mechanics and were susceptible of being handled mathematically and formulated in purely mechanical terms. The physical qualities of length, mass, and time that could be measured by a rule, weighed on a scale, and timed with a watch were the key factors in the mechanical conception of nature upon which the science and industry of that age hinged.

The entire weight of the empirical theory of natural knowledge rested upon the primary qualities. However, these suspension cables, which were anchored at one end in an unknowable substratum of substance and connected at the other end with purely subjective secondary qualities, provided extremely insecure supports for a theory of knowledge about reality.

If the primary qualities alone give authentic information about objective existences but these cannot divulge their inner nature to us, then how much can we actually know about the world around us? The rigid and untenable distinctions which Locke maintained between known qualities and unknowable substance, and between objectively existing primary qualities and purely subjective secondary ones, considerably cut down the extent of human knowledge. Locke declared that our knowledge of the world was mediocre, enough for our everyday affairs but not very comprehensive or profound. Mankind was condemned to "incurable ignorance."

With the sturdy common sense of the complacent bourgeois, Locke urged his fellow men to be satisfied with enough knowledge to get along in the ordinary business of life.

> All our business lies at home. Why should we think ourselves hardly dealt with that we are not furnished with compass and plummet to sail and fathom that restless, unnavigable ocean of the universal matter, motion and space? There are no commodities to be brought from thence serviceable to our use, nor that will better our condition.

Superficial appearance and material reality

Mechanical science was an immense step forward for human thought. All further advances in natural science have had to build upon this achievement of bourgeois society in its rise. But the view of nature it presented was not an unqualified vindication of strict empiricism.

Unlike the science of ancient and medieval times, the new science of nature was based upon the verification of physical theories by experiments. Salvirati, a character speaking for Galileo himself (1564–1642) in the *Dialogues Concerning the Two Principal Systems of the World,* says "that one sole experiment, or concludent demonstration, produced on the contrary part, sufficeth to batter to the ground . . . a thousand . . . probable arguments." This demand that theoretical conclusions submit to the test of observation and experiment, this appeal to the facts as the court of last resort in science, was empiricism's great source of strength.

On the other hand, the methods and conclusions of the new science conflicted with familiar facts of everyday experience. According to Copernicus the daily rotation of the celestial sphere about the earth was only an appearance; the earth, like the other planets, really revolved around the sun in a circular orbit. The apparent movement of the sun, which contradicted this unobvious relation, was explained by the complete rotation of the earth about its axis every twenty-four hours.

Mechanics as well as astronomy developed in defiance of the direct testimony of the senses and demonstrated that phenomenal appearances often invert the essential reality. Aristotelian physics taught that all heavy bodies had a "natural" tendency to fall toward the center of the universe, which was identified by medieval thinkers with the center of the earth. All other motion was "unnatural" because it required a constant counterforce to produce and sustain it.

Galileo, however, asserted that a body remains at rest or continues to move in a straight line unless some outside force intervenes to change its course. This principle of inertia was not so close to familiar experience as Aristotle's theory of motion; we have no experience of bodies moving with absolutely constant speed or of things being permanently at rest or of any process going on forever. But experiment proved that Galileo's principle was far more in accord with the real movements of things and could explain them far better.

It is not obvious to direct inspection that the blood flows in a continuous one-way circuit of the body. Vesalius (1514–1564) and earlier anatomists supposed that the blood ebbed and flowed forwards and backwards in the veins and arteries. Harvey (1578–1657) discovered the real action of the human blood system by assuming that it functioned like a hydraulic system. He regarded the heart as a pump, the veins and arteries as pipes, the valves as mechanical valves, and the blood itself as a fluid like any other.

In these fields of science superficial phenomena were set aside as misleading and reinterpreted as contradictory manifestations of a hidden network of causal relations which produced them. The machinery of nature operated behind the scenes to generate the effects we observe, just as clockwork moves the hands on the face of the clock. The task of science was to probe through the outward expressions which first impressed themselves upon our senses to the more remote and hidden materially active causes in the background.

The significant rational kernel in the distinction between the primary and secondary qualities adopted by Locke was the recognition that some properties and relations of things are more decisive in determining their natures than others, that reality consists of endless aspects of existences, and that science progresses by uncovering ever deeper layers of determining factors.

The new mechanical method did provide a deeper insight into the operations of nature and a greater control over them. But this extension of the knowledge of nature also produced new problems for the theory of knowledge. What were the relations between these underlying realities revealed by mechanics and formulated in mathematical terms and our subjective impressions of them? Which was the reality and which the appearance, the world of scientific objects and relations or the world of sights, sounds, colors, of our sense experience?

Neither the mechanical scientists nor the empirical philosophers succeeded in finding a satisfactory solution to this perplexing problem of reconciling the outward show of events with the driving forces behind them. Their answers swung from one extreme to the other. The more rationalist-minded tended to exalt the principles and laws of science as the expression of a supersensible reality, while the concrete sensory impressions were discounted as mere appearances. The empirically inclined viewed the generalized concepts as mere abstractions compared to the given evidence of the senses.

The first thinkers who undertook to examine the functioning of the capitalist economy encountered parallel difficulties in explaining the connections between appearance and reality. In England these were sometimes one and the same people since Locke, Berkeley, and Hume concerned themselves with analyzing money, commodities, and prices as well as qualities, ideas, and knowledge.

The apparent movements and relations of capitalism are very different from their real nature. To the superficial observer it looks as though the worker receives from the employer payment in full for his work. If this were really so, if there were an equal exchange of wages for labor and its products, then what would be the incentive for capitalist production and where would the profits of the capitalist come from?

The monetary transaction between the employer and the wageworker disguises the real relation between them. What appears on the surface as a relation of equality (the worker sells his "labor" to the employer for a mutually agreed upon price—if he does not like the price the employer offers, he need not work for that employer) is *in reality* a relation of inequality. The task of scientific investigation is to go from the phenomenal, superficial forms in which the relations directly present themselves, to the hidden *causes* which constitute their inner reality.

To those who stick to the semblances of economic relations, these internal workings of the capitalist system, discovered by political economy, seem grey, unsubstantial, and irrelevant mere abstractions. They are indeed abstractions for the very reason that they disregard the accidental, accessory circumstances and select what is *essential* in determining the phenomena under investigation. But abstractions are the tools for unlocking the workings of the real, "practical" world. Correct abstractions are generalized formulations of the more profound realities which lurk in the background and produce the immediately experienced but contradictory appearances of things.

The peculiar nature of capitalist social relations influenced the conceptions of the world evolved by the mechanical empiricists. Both mechanical science and bourgeois economics approached the respective spheres of existence they studied in order to penetrate beneath their phenomenal aspects and expose the concealed causal forces which generated them. Mechanical science disclosed certain important mainsprings of material movement in the solar system, in the actions of masses on earth, in the physiology of the human body. Classical political economy discovered some of the secrets of money as the depository of value and ultimately found the substance of value itself in labor. But the conceptions of the world of nature held by the mechanists and of the world of commodities held by the most perceptive bourgeois economists were inescapably narrow. They did not pass beyond the historical limitations of the society in which they lived.

How bourgeois thought views objective reality

Capitalism in its rise fostered a special type of mentality which had contrary characteristics. On the one hand, the creative bourgeois thinkers proved far more capable than their medieval and ancient predecessors of developing and employing abstract thought to probe through the phenomenal world to its underlying general structure. On the other hand, their thinking was dominated by the fetishistic worship of abstract quantity as the primordial feature and cardinal category of material reality.

These two characteristics are conspicuous in Locke's analysis of the external world into three aspects: unknowable material substances, objectively existing primary qualities which are exclusively quantitative in character, and subjective secondary qualities. How could the empiricist Locke have adopted a view of the world in which the realities of things were so utterly at odds with their everyday appearances?

Locke lived in the atmosphere of a thriving mercantile capitalism. The merchant capitalist had to look behind the use-value of commodities to what was essential in them—their exchange value. He saw the latter first of all as quantitative. Commodities do not appear on the market in their natural state as things with diverse specific and useful qualities. They are appraised, bought and sold only as so many distinct amounts of homogeneous and abstract value. This social property of value is exclusively quantitative; it embodies so much expended labor time. Value is made palpable through money, which functions as the means by which its quantity can be measured and compared.

This type of relation not only dominates the economic calculations of the capitalist system but also the higher intellectual activities of its philosophical representatives. The whole world comes to be conceived in similar terms of abstract quantities. Just as the objects of social existence acquire reality in the market only through their quality of abstract value expressed in definite sums of money, so the objects of nature seem to have reality only in their purely mechanical properties expressed as definite magnitudes in mathematical formulas.

To make this point clearer, imagine a department store stocked with goods from all over the world. This display of material wealth, however, exists as such only for the consumer. All these articles of use and enjoyment have a very different meaning to the owner of the establishment. To his capitalist eyes their aesthetic and useful characteristics are negligible. The objects count only as so many amounts of money-capital. Their value, expressed by their price tags, is their sole reality.

In a similar way, all the rich variety of material forms, forces, properties, and relations impress the mechanist, not in their immediate natural guises, but as so many quantities of identical units of such primary qualities as mass, motion, weight, etc. In this conception of the world, homogeneous quantity rules like an absolute monarch at the expense of the manifold diverse qualities of things.

The real things which exist in both nature and society are stripped of all those concrete qualities which do not fit into the fundamental relations and categories of the mechanical or the capitalist systems. These residual qualities are set aside as secondary, superfluous, merely subjective. Nature is deprived of its infinite abundance and diversity of real determinations, just as society's concrete wealth is obscured by exchange relations.

This emphasis upon the quantitative aspect of things was necessary for the advancement of science. Today it is a commonplace that the progress of scientific knowledge depends upon increasing accuracy of measurement. But in Locke's time this procedure was a revolutionary novelty with immense untapped consequences for theory and practice. The social sciences as well as the main branches of physical science received a powerful impetus from the application of precise measurement by quantitative methods. This same period witnessed the compilation of the first indices in political economy and the first essays in the tabulation of vital statistics.

Thus science, bourgeois economy, and the empirical philosophy shared a common preoccupation with the measurable properties of things. The coldness and greyness of bourgeois science has often been unfavorably contrasted with the warm, multicolored world of medieval religion. This inhumanity is not inherent in science but was a reflection of its bourgeois form of development and of the emotional attitude that capitalism inspired in its adherents. At the same time it must be recognized that a certain ruthlessness and callousness were required for the violent break they had to make from feudalism and scholasticism.

The same tools of thought which the early bourgeois scientists devised to probe into nature were used to inquire into the operations of capitalism. Although the early economists undertook their investigations the better to build a wealthy society, that is, to enrich the bourgeoisie, the social sciences benefited.

What we now call "classical" political economy arose. It discovered that value is not only quantitative but qualitative—and that its peculiar quality comes from labor. This discovery coincided with a higher stage in capitalist development: the organization of workshops by the merchant capitalists and their conversion into industrial capitalists.

Locke was the spokesman and herald of this development in England. As Marx noted, John Locke "was an advocate of the new bourgeoisie in all forms, the manufacturers against the working class and paupers, the commercial class against the old-fashioned usurers, the financial aristocracy against the state debtors, and . . . went so far as to prove in his own work that the bourgeois reason is the normal human reason." (*A Contribution to the Critique of*

Political Economy, p. 93)

The bourgeois bent of Locke's mentality accounted not only for the fundamental features of his inquiries but also for their limitations. In both the philosophical system of empiricism and the economic system of capitalism the inner essence of things remained enigmatic to the bourgeois mind. Substance in the mechanical system was as mysterious as the essence of value and the secrets of its monetary form were to the capitalist theoreticians. However much Locke strove to introduce rationality into his conceptions of nature and society, his inquiring mind, great as it was, had to retire baffled before these impenetrable sanctuaries of the bourgeois epoch.

3

Religion and metaphysics in Locke's philosophy

The bourgeois character of Locke's thought is no less evident in the way he conceived of religion and its relations with natural science.

The revolution which gave supremacy to the British bourgeoisie not only subordinated the sovereign to parliament but transformed the Anglican church into a supplementary agency of its government. These institutional readjustments found their reflections in religious thought. The traditional dogmas, based on revelation and philosophically justified by innate ideas, were challenged and displaced by a simplified and rationalized theology appealing to naturalistic arguments. Puritanism gave birth to Deism, the doctrine that God is the impersonal first cause of a thoroughly lawful nature.

Paradoxically, it was Hobbes, the champion of absolutism in government, who led the way in undermining the old supports of religion and transferring it to a different theoretical foundation. Hobbes deprived religion of its halo of sanctity by characterizing it as a product of men's ignorance and fears. Like Plato, Cicero, and other patricians of antiquity, he considered religion most useful in curbing seditious inclinations in the "multitude" and enhancing their loyalty to the established regime.

Hobbes thus transformed religion from a God-given revelation into a social cement. He came close to identifying the Kingdom of God with the kingdoms of Charles and James. The Sovereign on high backed up the sovereign on earth.

At the same time his mechanical philosophy, which took matter in motion as the fundamental reality, was essentially incompatible with the claims of religion. Pressed to its logical conclusions, the mechanical system of nature excluded God, the immortal soul, and other articles of the Christian creed. Clerics and scholars pounced upon these antisupernatural aspects of Hobbes' teachings and assailed him for perverting morals and religion as well as polluting politics. The outcries of these watchdogs against his "atheism," which endangered Hobbes' life at the time of the London Fire on September 2, 1666, alerted the ruling classes to the subversive implications of the mechanical conception for religion, morality, and the security of the state.

The victorious bourgeoisie needed institutions of the Christian faith to uphold their regime, just as they had to foster natural science to promote their material interests. But they could not maintain the same sort of religion as the absolute monarchy. They sought a religion tailored to their special requirements, a utilitarian Protestantism which blessed the union of Church and State, tolerated a certain degree of nonconformism, and reconciled the new findings of physical science with the religious viewpoint.

Locke's 'new model' religion

Locke undertook such a revision of religion in his book on *The Reasonableness of Christianity* as part of his task of formulating a theoretical outlook for the new capitalist rulership. As a liberal mediator, he steered a course between the more extreme conclusions of Hobbes, the monarchist materialist, and the religious conservatives. In broadening the scope of religious tolerance the Latitudinarian Locke had to trim the Church creed to a few essentials. He shelved some of the more objectionable dogmas of Catholicism like the Trinity, and justified those doctrines he retained by shifting the grounds for believing in them. For orthodox revelation backed up by innate ideas he substituted more naturalistic arguments proper to a "commonsense" religion.

This rationalization of Protestantism came easily to Locke. Like his friends Boyle and Newton, he was a devout believer, as eager to defend Christianity as to advance science and philosophy. Any suggestion that mechanical views could lead to religious skepticism was abhorrent to them. Boyle argued in a book called *The Christian Virtuoso* that "by being addicted to experimental philosophy a man is rather assisted than indisposed to be a good Christian."

How did these pious empiricists weave theology and physics into a single fabric? They accomplished this feat by interpreting nature and its laws, disclosed by scientific investigation, as the handiwork of God. The feudal mind had pictured God as an absolute sovereign whose providence directed all creation in accord with the Highest Good. These bourgeois minds conceived a divinity with the combined functions of a capitalist, a craftsman, and a constitutional monarch. God was no longer the Supreme Final Cause of the universe, as he was in scholastic metaphysics, but its First Efficient Cause. The cosmos was an immense machine invented by God to which, like a capitalist-machinist, he gave the original impulse. Once nature had been set into motion, it proceeded automatically according to the mechanical laws of material movement.

The functions of the formerly omnipotent God of the Middle Ages were thereby curtailed like those of the British monarchy. Both sovereigns were bound by the laws of the realm: the divinity by natural law, the monarchy by constitutional custom. These limited powers were supposed to interfere in the regular course of events only for emergency repairs and on state occasions.

To the reverent empiricists, nature's mechanism was a mirror of God's existence. Newton thought that space was "the sensorium of God." The harmonious working of the cosmic machine and the fit of its component parts according to mechanical law testified to God's design, His benevolence toward humanity, His perfection. And the farther science probed into the operations of nature, the more marvelous did the ingenuity of the divine artisan appear to them.

The unstable compromise between religion and science

In this way the new mechanical conception of nature became hitched to the traditional supernatural being. However, this forced union of opposing tendencies was an uneasy one which was periodically challenged from different sides. The more consistent mechanists noted the incongruity of a self-sustaining nature relying upon an underemployed God. This was tersely expressed in the next century when Laplace, the perfector of astronomical physics, was asked by Napoleon what place God had in his system. He replied: "Sire, I have no need for that hypothesis."

In his own day Locke's critics on the right accused him

of giving aid and comfort to the atheists. Dr. William Sherlock pointed out, for example, that Locke's denial of innate ideas banished "Original Mind and Wisdom out of the World" and made "Mind younger than Matter, later than making of the World, and therefore not the Maker of it."

Locke's positions that substance exists (even though it cannot be intimately known), that sensation is the basis of knowledge, and that matter might think, were closely akin to materialism. These elements in Locke's philosophy encouraged more thoroughgoing materialist conclusions. His influence in that direction can be most clearly seen in the writings of John Toland, of the deist Anthony Collins, and in the sensationalist and materialist schools of eighteenth-century France. But Locke himself did not take a stand firmly and fully upon materialist grounds.

For all its intrinsic inconsistency and incredibility, the synthesis of mechanical science and diluted Protestantism devised by the empirical thinkers of that epoch worked for two and a half centuries. The mechanical theology has served the British bourgeoisie in the sphere of religion as long and as well as its compromise with the monarchy and aristocracy has in politics. This unnatural ideological amalgam has not lost its hold upon the conservative British mentality to this very day. There are many Labour Party leaders who, although they profess to be socialists, have views on religion little different from Locke's.

Mechanical empiricism and metaphysical thinking

The mixture of natural science with Protestant piety was accompanied by a comparable blend of empirical knowledge and metaphysical notions in Locke's philosophy. The pioneer empiricists from Bacon to Hume squarely counterposed their new methods of thought to the vices of metaphysical abstraction. They condemned the metaphysics of scholasticism as the root of all evil, which they sought to remove by referring all ideas to their "originals" in sense impressions. Hume, for example, went so far as to urge that any book containing a priori reasoning about the nature of reality be committed "to the flames; for it can contain nothing but sophistry and illusion."

The vigorous polemics of the empiricists against scholastic metaphysics went far to destroy its influence. The empiricists thereby believed they had rid philosophy forever of such pernicious false reasoning. They were mistaken. They did get rid of medieval errors only to become caught in new metaphysical traps set for them by the mechanical view of nature and its modes of reasoning.

This does not mean that philosophy achieved no progress in the transition from scholasticism to empiricism. Even with its metaphysical aberrations, the method and postulates of the mechanical school were of a higher type which provided the theoretical scaffolding for a more correct and penetrating insight into reality. They represented as great a step forward in intellectual activity as the adoption of capitalist methods in place of feudal ones did in economic life. But just as the new forces of material production were still motivated by exploitation, so this progressive philosophy remained entangled in metaphysics.

All thinking proceeds by means of abstractions. Through images the mind constructs an inner mental world that reflects in its own way the perceptible outer physical world. Like a scene or sound recorded on a small section of magnetic tape, a given impression is fragmentary. As a recording it is also necessarily static. These are not defects of the thinking process; they constitute its basis.

The defect known as metaphysical thinking comes at the next stage when these recordings are used to interpret reality. First of all, since the images are perceptual they cannot directly reveal the basic structure of reality. This structure has to be inferred and tested indirectly. Secondly, reality is in motion. Even while a static impression is taken, reality has already changed and thereby somewhat invalidated the impression as a true reflection of what now exists. Thirdly, the interpretation or meaning of our stock of images is powerfully influenced by the society we live in. Instead of seeing reality as it is, we tend to see what a given society or class supposes reality to be.

A genuinely scientific thinker tries to rectify these aberrant tendencies by recognizing the static sides of his own thinking and by seeking the relations extending throughout the whole "tape." These relations reflect, to one degree or another, the relations of the outer world, a world in motion.

A metaphysician, on the other hand, fails to grasp these special traits of thought and thereby easily falls victim to a static outlook, particularly if this accords with the economic and political interests of his class. Thus the metaphysician, whose mentality is dominated by single images or formulas, imposes these upon reality. He projects an arbitrary conceptual framework upon the world, substitutes imaginary relations for real ones, pushes aside or is blind to facts that contradict his figments of fancy, and has great difficulty dealing with problems involving change, evolution, and development.

There are many such nonempirical elements in the empirical theory of knowledge and its view of the world. Here we can discuss only a few of the most important.

The most glaring instance of metaphysical thinking about thought among the empiricists from Locke to Hume was their belief that the highest type of knowledge was not derived from the empirical source of sense experience at all! They held that the most certain, perfect, and logical knowledge came from the direct intuition of the mind.

Here we can observe the combined influences of the mechanical-mathematical philosophy and religious idealism at work upon Locke. The mechanical conception accorded the paramount place in its instruments of knowledge to mathematics, and especially to geometry. Mathematics provided the indispensable concepts for formulating the physical relations essential to scientific explanation.

In line with this, the sober empiricists, Locke and Hume, assumed a fetishistic attitude toward mathematics. They were fascinated, as so many others have been before and since, by the power of its method which apparently proceeded by logical steps from perfectly "clear and simple" ideas to necessary conclusions without essential reference to the external world. They inconsistently maintained that mathematics, the model of perfect knowledge, depended upon pure reasoning alone and was in no way contingent upon matters of fact, that is, upon impressions and ideas rooted in objective relations and corresponding to them.

Thus, despite his initial opposition to innate principles, Locke concluded that the mind can know self-evident propositions of a mathematical and logical kind, such as "three are more than two and equal to one and two," and that these are directly discoverable by intuition alone. However, to base either general principles or particular judgments upon self-evidence alone is a method proper to rationalism and idealism, but not to a consistent empiricism.

Such an overevaluation of mathematical reasoning and admission of self-evident truths is necessarily coupled with a devaluation of the validity of ideas drawn from sensory sources. According to Locke, the purely deductive systems of ideas in mathematics were the sole source of absolutely certain knowledge. Merely empirical ideas, even those of the primary qualities, gave only probable knowledge. This, too, was far more rationalistic than empirical.

The motives underlying Locke's disregard of his own basic principle become plainer when we note that Locke extended this a priori method from mechanics and mathematics to morality. He contended that measures of right and wrong, which are among the most variable phenomena in human history, were absolute and could be deduced from self-evident universal propositions which were as unassailable as the axioms of mathematics.

This assertion of inflexible moral standards was a defensive reflex against the moral relativism set forth by the materialist Hobbes. As a spokesman for the conservatized bourgeoisie, Locke favored a cast-iron morality that could bulwark religion against skepticism and armor the new social and political regime against its plebeian critics.

Locke also needed the aid of an infallible intuition in his theory of knowledge to compensate for the weaknesses of its links with the objective world. For Locke we have immediate intuitive certainty of one thing only: our own existence. External existence, on the other hand, "is not altogether so certain as our intuitive knowledge, or the deductions of our own reason employed about the clear abstract ideas of our own minds." It would not take many steps to arrive at subjective idealism from such a starting point, although Locke himself did not drive in that direction. Berkeley did a little later.

Locke's separatism

Another pronounced metaphysical trait of Locke's thinking was its separatism. This runs all through his mechanical empiricism, from his version of nature to his interpretation of ideas. In Locke's view of nature only particular things exist; in society the isolated individual is the primary reality; in the human mind simple self-sufficient ideas are the basic units out of which knowledge is compounded.

Since Locke starts with dissociated particles, individuals, and ideas, the problem then arises in all the domains of existence: how do these originally independent entities come together? The single principle of unification in his empiricism is mechanical aggregation by way of arithmetical addition. The atoms constitute material aggregates which have only external relations with one another; individuals combine into social groupings and set up governments by means of a contract; the simple ideas which are the elementary components of thought make up complex ideas by way of association.

This radical separatism does not arise from direct empirical observation; it is the product of analytical abstraction which mistakes its one-sided conclusions for the real conditions of existence. Material particles do not exist, nor are they ever experienced, in total isolation from one another; they are constituents of a network of natural relations in constant interaction. People never function by themselves in history, but always as members of some concrete collective body of producers. Even the most elementary ideas are organically connected with other ideas in consciousness, as well as with their material conditions and objective counterparts in reality.

In Locke's philosophy, however, the single thing is severed from its context in nature; the individual from his social-historical kind; the singular from the general. In this way the universal relations of things become dissolved from concrete realities into mere abstractions; the necessary social bonds of people become arbitrary; and the general aspects of concepts become conventional names useful for identification but not necessarily reflecting any essential features of the nature of things.

All parts of this metaphysical outlook of the classical

empiricists hang together: its one-sided atomism in nature; its absolute individualism in society; its totally discrete ideas in the mind. Phenomena are not viewed in their basic internal relationships and processes of development but are torn out of their universal connections and incessant transformations.

Such a conception of nature, society, and thought processes, which takes the independent and exclusive unit for its foundation and starting point, is bourgeois to the core. As Marx pointed out, the totally isolated individual, Robinson Crusoe on his island, is one of the dominant illusions of the capitalist epoch. It is an ideological fantasy reflecting the exchange relations of mutually independent producers under conditions of free competition. Although tightly bound by the social-economic ties which regulated his life and thought, the bourgeois imagined himself as a free-floating force subject to "natural" economic laws but with only incidental bonds to the rest of society.

Bourgeois thought is thoroughly permeated with this metaphysics of individualism. It is essentially a translation into religion, politics, and related fields of culture of the conditions of commodity-producing society. This individualism was carried to its extreme in the Puritan theology shared by Locke. There the solitary soul has secret communion with God and receives grace directly from Him without mediation through any third party, priest, pope, or clerical institution. Religion becomes a purely private transaction between the possessor of an immortal soul and his God, just as the act of buying and selling takes place between the private owners of commodities and money.

The theory of bourgeois democracy

This theory of individual rights in religion (church democracy) went hand in hand with the doctrine of individual rights in law and politics (state democracy). The banner of militant democracy was most fully unfurled at the height of the Puritan Revolution by the Levellers and the Agitators of Cromwell's Model Army whose program urged full freedom for religion, a constitutional republic, an end to monopolistic privilege in the economy, and other reforms. Locke watered down the robust radical program of these plebeian forces into a moderate liberalism which suited the taste of the victorious, upper-class Whigs at the close of the revolutionary epoch.

Locke was the outstanding theoretician—and metaphysician—of a constitutionalized bourgeois government. Since his time this formalized and restricted type of representative democracy has become sanctified as the creed of liberalism. Its principal tenets are supposed to be irreproachable and unquestionable, although they can no more be detached from social evolution and class interests or exempt from materialist criticism than the premises of laissez-faire capitalism itself. In fact, the two are organically connected.

In the historical sequence of ideological development in the Western world, *bourgeois* democracy takes its place as a rationalized and secularized offspring of Christian teachings on equality. The Gospels taught that all men, regardless of their social status, are equal in the sight of God. This purely religious equality of the slave and the slave-owner, the lord and the serf, the oppressor and the oppressed, the rich and the poor was viciously fictitious. Despite its consoling conclusions, in earthly reality, the slave remained in chains, the poor went hungry, and the humble, however exalted in the afterlife, continued to suffer degradation in this one.

The advocates of bourgeois democracy translated this mystical demand for equality into prosaic legal and political terms by means of the theory of natural law. By the decree of nature (or reason) all men were equal before the law and should have equal voice and vote in deciding the destiny of their country. In the mythology of the natural-law theorists, these rights were inherent and inalienable and were supposedly used to constitute their original government through a social compact.

According to Locke, the people retained the power to replace their form of government whenever they felt that the original agreement between the ruler and ruled had been abrogated. This political credo was used to justify the displacement of the absolute monarchy by the constitutional regime controlled by the bourgeois parliament. But it was loaded with high explosives.

The Levellers had already wielded this doctrine of revolutionary democracy, not only against the Monarchy and the Established Church, but also against the conservative Presbyterian Long Parliament and Cromwell's military dictatorship. It could easily become the weapon of any popular movement directed against a tyrannical regime. This was demonstrated a century later when the leaders of the colonial revolt in North America, tutored by Locke, turned his arguments against British rule. Ironically, in both America and France, the liberal Locke became the theoretical inspirer of revolutionary causes.

The progressive content of Locke's individualism was uppermost in the struggles waged against feudal forces for equal suffrage, personal liberties, freedom of conscience, and other principles of democracy. Its reactionary and mystical aspects moved to the fore once capitalist sovereignty had become entrenched in economic and political life.

Parliamentary democracy was raised upon two pillars. One was the *fiction* that the prevailing inequality of social and economic conditions had no decisive effects upon the *ideal* equality of legal and political rights. Along with it went the *reality* of the absolute right of private property.

Locke himself was a staunch defender of bourgeois property interests. In his *Treatise of Civil Government* he intermingles all the basic rights of individuals with the concept of property ownership, the preservation of "their lives, liberties *and estates.*"

Locke's theorizing accorded with his practice. He personally profited from the slave trade. As Secretary of the Board of Trade and Plantations, he helped frame a constitution for the Carolinas on the Atlantic seacoast which was expressly designed to prevent "a numerous democracy" from developing and which concentrated all powers in the feudal proprietors. He advocated cruel punishments for paupers and the laboring poor in both Virginia and England.

For the liberal bourgeois—as for the petty-bourgeois liberals—the unqualified, eternal standards of parliamentary democracy presumably stood above the economic realities and class distinctions of capitalist society. However much this pleased the big property-owners, it did not calm the outraged sense of justice among the poor and the propertyless. Although they may not have been able to give a theoretical or historical explanation of the fraud, the workers were well aware that something was radically wrong with a democracy in which ten thousand had to labor incessantly so that ten might live luxuriously.

In opposition to this limited democracy of the bourgeois regime, the plebeian forces headed by the working class later demanded the real fulfillment of democratic principles and promises. This movement for genuine social equality and the expansion of democracy, counterposed to the rule of the propertied parliamentarians, found its fullest expression during the nineteenth century in the program of socialism.

So far as political democracy is concerned, the task of the revolutionary socialist movement was to promote the processes of democratization, initiated by the bourgeois revolution, to their logical conclusions. The economic and political conditions for accomplishing this were the conquest of power by the working class which would abolish exploitation and achieve equality by expropriating the capitalists, nationalizing the major means of production, and planning the economy. This collectivist conception of *workers' democracy* became the progressive class alternative to the "possessive individualism" and restricted, bourgeoisified democracy promulgated by Locke.

Meanwhile, the abstract individualism of Locke's school was to become converted into its opposite. What was once a lever for increasing freedom turned into an obstacle to its extension. Bourgeois individualism came to serve as a cover for unrestrained exploitation and the perversion of democratic institutions by reactionary ruling classes. In the United States, for example, "free enterprise" became a watchword of monopoly rule and "democracy" a screen for imperialist policy. In England the abstraction of "individual liberty" is the main excuse put forward by middle-class liberals for opposing socialism, and by right-wing reformists in the labor movement for justifying their collaboration with the representatives of capitalism and refusing to complete the nationalization of industry or to concentrate power in the hands of the working people, the majority of the nation.

4

Berkeley's inversion of empiricism

Locke had a wide range of disciples and descendants. These branched out in divergent directions and some wound up in opposing camps. This was the logical outcome of the inconsistencies and incompleteness of empiricism.

From its birth empiricism was an unstable compound of materialist and idealist elements, the result of a compromise between the two antithetical standpoints on the key problem of philosophy: the relation between thought and being. The double-barreled concept of "experience" which expressed the object-subject relation could serve as a springboard for materialist or idealist conclusions, depending on which side of the relation was made predominant. Just as water can be dissociated by electrolysis into hydrogen and oxygen, so empiricism came to be separated into materialism and idealism, according to the motives and manner of interpreting its central concept.

Sensationalism

The materialist stream of thought in England flowed from Bacon and Hobbes through Locke. Bacon had no doubt that sense experience gave true information about the world and was in fact the only reliable source of human knowledge. Hobbes, his continuator, insisted that material things alone were perceptible and knowable; God existed but the fact could not be proved. Despite the residual metaphysical and religious elements in Locke's philosophy, the main line of his theory of knowledge on this point was similar to that of his predecessor Bacon and his contemporary Hobbes. Simple ideas are valid because they correspond to the things that produce them.

This side of empiricism was refined and reinforced by an array of eighteenth-century materialist thinkers in England and France. The most radical among them took Locke's proposition that all knowledge was derived from sense data and simplified it to the extreme. Locke had not done this. He held that knowledge could be attained in three ways: through sensation, reflection, and intuition.

The French priest Etienne de Condillac (1715–1780) rejected intuition and reduced reflection to sensation. In his chief work (*Traité des sensations,* 1754) he attempted to show that the functions and forms of thought were nothing but the transformations of simple passive sensations. He invoked the imaginary model of a statue whose senses were awakened to activity one after another under the influence of external impressions to illustrate how humans acquire their original faculties and develop the whole content of their consciousness and knowledge out of sensations and their comparisons.

This doctrine of sensationalism was the most one-sided materialist offspring of Locke's empiricism. It inspired such French Encyclopedists as Helvetius, La Mettrie, Diderot, and Holbach as well as various empirical schools on both shores of the Atlantic during the eighteenth and nineteenth centuries.

Berkeley's idealism

Empiricism was piloted into an altogether different channel by George Berkeley (1683–1753), who combated those tendencies of his age which undermined religious belief by explaining phenomena in terms of matter and motion. He transmuted empiricism into idealism by denying the independent reality of the material world and its effects upon ourselves. His work was facilitated by the axiom of Locke's theory of knowledge that the mind "has no other *immediate* object but its own ideas." From this it followed that objects in the physical world are not directly experienced nor are their existence and operations immediately known. They are inferred by our minds from our impressions or ideas.

Locke did not doubt that such inference, which we make all the time in our everyday activities, gives valid, if limited, knowledge of objective reality. Bishop Berkeley disputed this. Locke was inconsistent, he argued. If we perceive nothing but complexes of sensible qualities, it is illegitimate to jump from these to the independent existence of any causal entities behind or beyond them. Sense data have no existence apart from our perception of them. The existence of objects consists simply and solely in their being perceived.

To the question, What happens to things when there is no one present to perceive them? Berkeley responds: In that case they are in the mind of God, who gives these perceptions to us in the first place.

Berkeley stood empiricism on its head by expunging

the last traces of materiality from it. Whereas Bacon and Hobbes made substance, body, or nature the prime cause of our sensations, ideas, and knowledge, Berkeley brought in God as their ultimate author. Whereas the materialists insisted on the *unity* of thought and being, Berkeley completely absorbed all being into thought and thus made these opposites identical. Whereas the empiricism of the materialist-minded Locke had pushed back religion to make more room for science, Berkeley converted the empirical epistemology into a weapon for demolishing the foundations of science and discrediting materialism, skepticism, and atheism in order to reestablish the shaken supremacy of revealed religion.

Berkeley directed his polemic against all those constituents of Locke's doctrines that lent support to mechanical materialism. Locke's *An Essay Concerning Human Understanding* was based on four propositions. 1) The physical world consists of substance which we know nothing about except that it is there. 2) This substance contains certain inherent qualities (size, shape, speed, number, solidity) with which science deals. 3) These primary qualities produce some ideas in our minds which are copies of themselves and other secondary qualities (colors, tastes, smells, temperatures, sounds) which do not resemble anything in external objects. 4) The mind has the power to form abstract ideas from particular experiences. These generalizations are in the last analysis conceptual modifications of the materials passively received from sensation and organized by reflection.

Berkeley controverted all these assertions. He denied that substance exists or functions as the physical matrix of any qualities whatever; that there is any categorical distinction between the qualities we perceive; or that we possess abstract general ideas.

The main target of his attack was the materialist underpinning of Locke's position, his doctrine of substance as a hidden, inert, and unreachable substrate of phenomena. Berkeley argued that matter did not exist because it can neither be perceived by the senses nor apprehended by the mind. Nothing can be held to exist apart from our perceptions. And if "to be is to be perceived," unperceived bodies do not exist.

Berkeley justified this pure phenomenalism on the ground that sensations and ideas could not be derived from something so utterly unlike themselves as the passive, negative, inaccessible, and unknowable entity Locke defined substance to be. The two things had nothing in common with one another. Belief in the reality of substance was an unwarranted act of blind faith.

Berkeley was enabled to rule out the objective reality of substance with some plausibility as a result of the extremely inadequate conception of matter fostered by mechanical physics, which pictured matter as impenetrable, immobile, and immutable. For Locke the underlying substance which was the repository of the primary qualities, the generator of the secondary ones, and the ultimate cause of sensations was not endowed with any powers and was destitute of all inner processes. How could so passive a cause produce the diversity of perceptions that people experience, Berkeley asked.

This defect in the mechanical interpretation of matter was first offset by the free-thinking Irish follower of Locke, John Toland. In his *Letters to Serena* (1704) he maintained that motion must be considered as an equally original and essential property of matter as extension and solidity. God created matter active. There is motion everywhere in nature; it only appears to the senses as if at certain points there were cessation and rest. Deeper inquiry will uncover internal energy, self-movement in all things. But Locke deprived substance of motion, and this disregard for the inner dynamism of things strengthened Berkeley's arguments against the existence of material substance.

Berkeley's idealistic critique keenly analyzed and demolished Locke's disjunction between the primary qualities which are "patterns or images of things which exist without the minds, in an unthinking substance which they call *matter*" and the secondary which are strictly subjective although generated by the primary qualities. He noted that the two sets of qualities are always to be found together and both are equally dependent upon perception.

Berkeley correctly saw that qualities could not be divided into two opposing classes: one outside us and the other within us. However, from the fact that they must all be placed on the same existential footing, his idealism led to the illegitimate conclusion that they must be entirely within us. He thereby ignored the two-sided character of sensory qualities which have both an objective content produced by material causes and a subjective form of manifestation. Berkeley transformed perceptions, which are links between external realities and the living organism, into self-enclosed entities.

Along with corporeal substance and the objective aspect of qualities, Berkeley, anticipating Hume, banished physical causation from reality. Locke had defined a cause as that which produces any simple or complex idea, as heat generated fluidity in wax. Heat is the cause and fluidity the effect. Berkeley denied that there was any genetic connection between phenomena. One idea does not produce another; there is merely a symbolic relation between them. The heat is simply a signal that melting would follow. The two are joined only by mental association, not by material bonds. Berkeley leaned upon this notion of causation as a pure mental construct to further sever ideas from external objects.

Locke's theory of truth was founded on the causal production and genetic connection between ideas in the mind and corporeal realities, whatever the distances between them. For Locke our ideas represent the properties and relations of external things and are not utterly dependent on our minds.

Berkeley maintained that our impressions were too lively to be copies of inert external things and that no connection or correspondence could be established between two such disparate kinds of existences. We cannot go beyond or behind our sense impressions to objects which verify them.

Having expunged any substantial difference between ideas and real things, Berkeley could not have truth consist in their correspondence. His criteria of truth are thoroughly idealistic. The ideas in my mind are true if they resemble those of my fellow men and the objectivity, order, significance, and necessity of our common ideas depend upon their production and maintenance by the divine Author of nature, that Supreme Spirit who communicates with us through the universal language of sense symbols.

Berkeley did not leave the individual isolated amidst his sensations or ideas. Such solipsism would have run counter to the theological intent of his philosophizing. He granted that our impressions were dependent on a power other and greater than ourselves.

The other half of Locke's theory of substance enabled him to confer that all-important role on God. Locke taught that there were two eternal kinds of substance: corporeal and spiritual. Spirits are the only substances which are active, indivisible, and directly knowable. Once Berkeley had annulled material substance the way was cleared to make spiritual substance the sole source of our sensations and ideas.

A spirit is that which perceives, wills, and thinks. According to the Bishop, we humans are spiritual substances with an immortal and incorruptible soul. One spirit can act upon another since they are of the same kind. Thus in perception the divine spirit is impressed upon the minds of men. "Everything we see, hear, feel or anywise perceive by sense, being a *sign* or *effect* of the power of God: as is our perception of these very motions which are produced by men," Berkeley wrote.

Experience is the way by which God communicates with men. The mechanists believed that God created nature and men can learn about His wonders and wisdom through investigating the operations of nature. In Berkeley's spiritualism, nature is supplanted by God who possesses all the capacities that the passive, unfruitful, and mysterious substance of the materialists lacked. The divine power was active, productive, and known to us through perception and the mind as well as through revelation.

God excites sensations in us in a coherent order and His observing mind makes possible the continued existence of objects when no human perceives them. Thus the universe is composed, not of two modes of material being, nature and man, as consistent materialism contends, but of ourselves and God, two forms of spirit.

Berkeley resorted to God as the author of the order of experience and the necessary cause of our impressions in order to provide an unassailable warranty for Christian morals and Anglican theology. For example, he argued that miracles were possible on the ground that God can interfere with the order of things and reverse their ordinary behavior.

Berkeley's ultimate weapon against the existence of material substance was his nominalist theory of ideas. Locke had taught that the mind has the capacity to form generalizations by divesting the ideas impressed upon it by particular objects of all the adventitious circumstances which make these ideas resemble actual things, such as time, place, and other concomitant ideas. This power of abstraction is the exclusive prerogative of the human mind and is not shared with the animals.

Berkeley denied that there are any such things as abstract general ideas or that we can conceive of them. For example, he said, I cannot form an image of a triangle which is not some particular kind of triangle, oblique, rectangular, equilateral, etc. He here confused the psychological image, through which we visualize a concept, with its significant content which refers to the essential features of some class of objects.

Berkeley's insistence on the concrete particularity of experience did not give entirely negative results. He was among the first men of his time to detect the flaw in the conceptions of absolute time and absolute space which were the pillars of Newtonian physics. But he went from this brilliant recognition of the relativity of space to proclaim that space was an empty abstraction without any counterpart in reality because it corresponded to no immediate perception.

He likewise contended that substance was merely a word, an empty term, because it was void of any specific traits.

By refusing to go beyond the particularity of experienced things, Berkeley halted the process of knowledge at its initial and lowest level. Knowledge begins with the observation of separate and individual phenomena. But in the course of its development and deepening, the generalizing mind sets aside whatever is incidental and accidental in the mass of particulars and forms categories and formulates laws which reflect the common, fundamental, and decisive traits of things and their connections.

The concept of space is an abstraction from the diverse concrete spatial qualities and relations mankind has encountered. This generalization is not devoid of meaning or substance, as Berkeley contended, but a category containing the wealth of all those specific determinations of space which characterize objects and enter into experience.

The concept of matter reflects an equally essential aspect of reality. All sorts of things exist in their concrete interactions and interrelations. Matter or substance is a unified general term extracted by mental insight from the endless multiplicity of their diverse manifestations. However, it is a real and rational abstraction, not a purely null and imaginary one. The concept of matter has objective truth because it corresponds to the fundamental nature of reality. It affirms and indicates the objectivity of things, that indispensable common feature by which they exist and function on their own account independently of being perceived by anyone, human or divine.

Berkeley's idealism depended upon disqualifying this universal attribute of things which is the cornerstone of any form of materialism. The unmitigated spiritualism of disembodied perceptions in the minds of God and man, which Berkeley constructed to ward off the diffusion of irreligion, was itself more brittle than a stained-glass window. But his criticisms did bring to light vulnerable points in the premises of the empirical philosophy. These weaknesses were probed to the bottom by Berkeley's immediate successor, David Hume.

5

The skepticism of Hume

Certain spokesmen have performed a valuable service for the promotion of thought by pressing the basic principles of their viewpoint to the most extreme logical conclusions. David Hume (1711–1776) was such a philosopher.

Hume deepened the dissociation of the antithetical elements in the empirical synthesis by liquidating its supports in materiality and thereby casting it adrift on the waters of skepticism.

Locke had taught that all our knowledge is derived from sense experience; that we have nothing in our minds in the first instance but ideas; and that these are self-contained units. Berkeley had restricted the content of knowledge to our ideas. Accepting these propositions, Hume resolved to apply them with utmost rigor to the foundations of our knowledge.

We have the idea of permanent substances. What impression, Hume asks, does this idea come from? He looked for, but could not find, any direct sense perception which indicated the existence of material bodies. In that case the existence of an external world independent of our perceptions could not be demonstrated.

"Let us fix our attention out of ourselves as much as possible; let us chase our imaginations to the heavens, or to the ultimate limits of the universe; we never really advance a step beyond ourselves, nor can we conceive of any kind of existence, but the perceptions which have appeared in that narrow compass. This is the universe of the imagination, nor have we any idea but what is here produced," he wrote.

If we inquire, What is the source of these perceptions that arise in the imagination? Hume answers that it is impossible to decide whether they come from external objects, are produced in the mind, or by God. "As to these impressions, which arise from the senses, their ultimate cause is in my opinion, perfectly inexplicable by human reason," he says.

Hume follows up this divorce of sensory perceptions from their material conditions by denying that the idea of causality has any basis in objective reality. When we examine our sense impressions, they do not provide any evidence that one event has any necessary or essential connections with another or that one thing is instrumental in producing another. All that our experience enables us to say, or our reason to know, is that one thing follows another or accompanies another. But there is nothing given in our impressions to warrant the conclusion that one is the cause and the other the effect.

Hume did not stop with eliminating any basis for believing in the existence of material substance and the reality of the external world. He went beyond Berkeley to point out that there were no better grounds for believing in the existence of a permanent self, apart from the succession of our inner perceptions. Finally, he could find no sense impression which demonstrated the existence of God or the immortality of the soul.

Thus, operating with the empirical razor that we never really advance a step beyond our sense impressions, Hume slashed at the most indispensable convictions of our daily life and practical activity (that the world exists outside our sensations of it, that our memory can give us a true picture of the past, that we have integrated selves with an enduring identity). He removed the essential premises of scientific knowledge (that material things exist, that they are causally generated and connected, and that lawfulness governs their interrelations and movements). In addition, he pulled down the arguments of "natural theology" for the existence of God and immortality, without, however, repudiating religion entirely.

What remained of the foundations of knowledge after Hume's surgery? Nothing but what is immediately before us in sensation. Verifiable knowledge was contracted to the pinpoint of the individual's own impressions and ideas at the very moment of experiencing them. As Santayana has stressed in his book on *Skepticism and Animal Faith,* any consistent development of Hume's standpoint must end in solipsism, the fantastic position that nothing exists but the solitary individual, and then only at the present moment.

Having arrived at this point of no return to the objective world, Hume still had to explain why, if our beliefs in the reality of material bodies, the past, causation, and personal identity have no basis in sense experience and cannot withstand the tests of reason, they nevertheless arise in us all and persist so strongly. Hume attributed the origin and endurance of these beliefs to the instinctive and imaginative side of our nature, to our habit of associating one impression or idea with another, despite their inherently loose and separate character.

For example, the notion of causation does not depend upon any discoverable inner material bonds between one event or body and another. It is generated exclusively by the irrepressible and irresistible disposition of the human mind to couple whatever has appeared together constantly and regularly in the past so that we acquire the habit of expecting them to arrive together in the future. Although we generalize this expectation into a universal law of causation, this rule has no objective basis. It is a pure assumption, a matter of "animal faith," as Santayana terms it, which can be upset and nullified at any time.

Hume does not deny that our beliefs in material things, causation, the past, and personal identity are useful and even unavoidable. But he insists that at bottom they are simply and solely products of psychological association. Valuable as practical makeshifts, they have no basis in sense experience and no roots in objective reality. They are essentially irrational and ultimately inexplicable.

Hume's criticism marked a major turning point both in the evolution of empiricism and in the history of Western philosophy. He exposed to full view the intrinsic flaw in the empirical theory of knowledge where it feared or failed to take a firm and clear stand on whether sense experience gave valid knowledge of the reality of the external world. He called into serious question both the existence of that reality and the validity of our knowledge concerning it. At the same time Hume forced subsequent philosophers to give a rational explanation of how experience did provide genuine knowledge.

Hume's skepticism laid the basis for phenomenalism, positivism, empirio-criticism, pragmatism, agnosticism and similar mutations of empirical doctrine which were developed in the nineteenth and twentieth centuries. It gave a theoretical warrant for the subjectivism, impressionism, and other vices of thought which thereafter accompanied empiricism and its applications.

With Hume sense data for the first time became converted into "senseless data." According to Bacon, Hobbes, and to a lesser degree Locke, our sensations opened the door to knowledge of the world and enabled us to peer and penetrate into the nature of reality. For Hume our sensations do not serve as passageways for getting in touch with the world outside and learning about it but as barriers which cut off access to reality or knowledge about it. Instead of informing us of their real origins or being representative of their objects and referring to the external environment, sensations bring no news of the external world to us. They tell us only about themselves—and about ourselves. "The senses," Hume wrote, "are only the inlets through which these images are received, without being ever able to produce any immediate intercourse between the mind and the object."

Locke had maintained: "We have knowledge of our own existence by intuition; of the existence of God by demonstration [*i.e.*, by reason] and of other things by sensation." Hume denied the first two of these assertions and cast deep doubt upon the third.

By denying that the relation of cause and effect had any existence in events or in the connection of objects, Hume deprived science of any objective material basis. He could not find necessity or lawfulness anywhere in experience. There were no necessary connections between one thing and another, or between one idea and another, or between things and ideas. All these were held together only through associations imposed on them by custom.

By making causation into a purely subjective notion whereby the connections of things depended exclusively upon our habits of expectation and the associative powers of the mind, Hume shifted the whole weight of knowledge onto the subjective side. However, the solitary self is too weak to sustain so great a burden. Actually, if Hume's contentions were true, the entire structure of human knowledge would collapse for lack of support in objective reality.

Hume also laid the basis for the subsequent pragmatic conception of knowledge by treating ideas as habits or rules of behavior adopted for the practical needs of getting along in the world. In place of the "correspondence theory of truth," that ideas are valid if they agree in content with their objects, he put forward what can aptly be characterized as the "opportunist theory of truth." Since our most cherished ideas cannot find a basis and backing in an independent reality, then we must treat as true whatever enables us to get along best in everyday affairs. Truth, then, is determined not by the unity of the content of ideas with their references in the external world, but by purely practical considerations of expediency in conduct.

The outcome of Hume's *Enquiry Concerning Human Understanding* was exceedingly ironical. He began with the intention of finding out what sensory evidence there was for our fundamental beliefs about the world. He ended by detaching those beliefs from their foundations in objective reality.

He thus became the father of that impressionism which has attended empiricism since that time. Impressionism is a habit of thought which inclines to rely for its conclusions upon what is immediate and superficial rather than to dig for the fundamental causes behind appearances. It inflates accidental and second-rate factors at the expense of essential and primary ones, and seizes upon episodic rather than enduring elements in explaining a phenomenon. It ends with denying in effect any significant difference between these. Such methods of thought are encouraged by Humean skepticism, which doubts whether the underlying reality can be reached either through ordinary experience or generalizing thought and cultivates reliance upon whatever is closest at hand to solve the problems of life and of science.

Hume's radical empiricism operated in two different directions. On one side it undercut the arguments of the natural theologians in favor of divine providence and immutable rules of morality, which had propped up the dogmas of Protestantism. On the other side his views on substance and causality swept away the basis for the truths of natural and social science.

However, these contrary consequences of his skepticism did not exert equally enduring influence. The antireligious aspect of his criticism, which earned him the title of "the infidel Hume," was soon absorbed and rendered harmless. Although Hume exploded certain arguments of the theologians, his negations, like those of Kant, left room for accepting religion as a matter of faith.

But his disqualification of the reality of causation and his doubts about the existence of the external world have been saddled like a crushing weight upon the empirical school ever since.

After Hume, empiricism became tainted to the marrow with skepticism about the possibility of acquiring valid knowledge of the external world and even of the individual self. Hume's followers tried to find some way out of the trap of the solitary self and its purely private sense-impressions—but without success. Indeed, there could be no escape so long as they adhered to the original individualist and separatist presuppositions of the empirical epistemology.

This agnosticism gnawed like a worm within empiricism until it grew hollow to the core. In the voices of its pioneers like Bacon and Locke, empiricism had proclaimed confidence in the powers of the human mind to explore and know reality. Hume's skepticism corroded the internal ties of their synthesis of ideas. Thereafter empiricism doubted everything on principle, including its own value. It generated distrust of man's abilities to know the world, to know it truly, and to transform it surely through the guidance of such knowledge.

6

Nineteenth-century empiricism from Mill to Mach

After Hume empiricism forked off in two ways. Crossing the English Channel to Germany, Hume's criticism prodded Kant into the line of reasoning which produced his Critical Philosophy and led on to the Absolute Idealisms of Fichte, Schelling, and Hegel, which opposed the postulates of empiricism.

The eclecticism of John Stuart Mill

Staying at home, the skeptical sensationalism of Hume had a quite different sequel. It was succeeded by the Phenomenalism of John Stuart Mill (1806–1873), the Radical Utilitarian who was the outstanding figure of nineteenth-century British empiricism. In Mill the contradictions inherent in the empirical theory of knowledge became more explicit and its inconsistent and compromising character far more pronounced.

Mill, for example, defined matter as "the permanent possibility of sensation." This is a considerable retreat from Locke's views on the reality of objects in the external world. Mill made the existence of objects depend upon the *possibility* of their being perceived by us. This is a concession, not simply to Hume's skepticism, but to Berkeley's idealism which made the existence of objects depend upon their being *actually* perceived by us. Indeed, Mill did not hesitate to proclaim his agreement with Berkeley's school of subjective idealism.

To the materialist "the permanent possibility of sensation" depends upon the prior independent reality of physical existence. Mill could not make up his mind what, if anything, really preceded and produced sensations. He contended, for instance, that the external world was nothing but a succession of ideas which can be expected to recur regularly. This is a replica of the phenomenalism of Hume.

Then, in addition to this domain of appearance which is presumably all that we can experience, Mill turned about and posited the existence of another world of things as its substance and cause. In this sally he reverted to the position of Locke. But this outer world is neither known nor knowable. Here Mill embraced the figure of Kant with his doctrine of the unknowability of "things in themselves."

How, on Mill's initial premises that we have no immediate knowledge of objects but only of our own ideas and that the external world is nothing but a succession of regularly associated ideas, is any knowledge of this behind-the-scene world possible, or even its existence ascertainable?

With Mill the inconsistencies of Locke's theory of knowledge became crystallized into that systematic *eclecticism* which has marked all of latter-day empiricism. Eclecticism is that unsystematic tendency of thought which shuttles between antagonistic positions and becomes mired in outright contradiction. In seeking to reconcile what is irreconcilable, the eclectic accepts opposing views, disregards their incompatibility, and violates the inner harmony of his own teachings.

This fundamental characteristic of Mill's thought was noted by a contemporary critic, James Martineau, who wrote regarding Mill's theory of knowledge:

"On the one hand, we have found him resolving all our knowledge into self-knowledge; denying any cognitive access to either qualities or bodies external to us; and shutting us up with our own sensations, ideas and emotions. But, on the other hand, though we *know* nothing but the phenomena of ourselves we *are* nothing but phenomena of the world: the boast is vain of anything original in the mind; the sensations from which all within us begins are the results of *outward experience*. And thus we are landed in this singular result: our only sphere of cognizable reality is subjective: and *that* is generated from an objective world which we have no reason to believe exists. In our author's theory of *cognition*, the non-ego disappears in the ego; in his theory of *being*, the ego lapses into the non-ego. Idealist in the former, he is materialist in the latter." (*Essays*, iii. 520)

Mill's philosophy marks a decisive step in the decline of empiricism from its great and glorious era, just as his equally eclectic system of political economy was a decline in bourgeois thought compared to the classical work of Smith and Ricardo. Unnerved by Hume's skepticism and disarmed by Mill's surrender to the primary propositions of Berkeley's idealism, the degradation of empiricism has proceeded steadily from then on.

The empirio-positivism of Ernst Mach

Mill's phenomenalism led on to the empirio-criticism and positivism of the late nineteenth and twentieth centuries. These tendencies, starting from the premise that objects are nothing but combinations of sense data, cast doubt on our ability to know material reality and culminate in all kinds of quasi-idealistic conclusions.

Ernst Mach (1838–1916) played an ambivalent role at a crucial turning point in modern thought. On one side, his critical analysis of the flaws in the theoretical system of Newtonian mechanics, and especially its key categories of absolute space, time, and motion, proved to be important stimulants to the progress of physical science. Even though Einstein was not an adherent of his positivist philosophy, Mach's ideas were highly influential in the formation of Einstein's relativity theory.

On the other hand, Mach had a retrogressive effect in the field of philosophic method. This was pointed out by Lenin in his book, *Materialism and Empirio-Criticism,* written in 1908, which is a searching examination from the standpoint of dialectical materialism of the relativist agnosticism and idealism embedded in the theory of knowledge of Mach and his disciples.

Mach, for example, passes over from the proposition that *knowledge* consists of nothing but sensations, to the quite different assertion that the *world* consists solely of our sensations.

Mach's nonmaterialist standpoint can be gauged by the following assertion regarding bodies in the natural world. "To claim that there are in nature the objective counterparts of this conceptual apparatus is an unjustifiable piece of metaphysics; we may find the concept of a body, for example, useful, but we must not allow ourselves to think that there are bodies in the natural world; we experience only sensations."

Over the past three centuries, the empirical school has exhibited an ever stronger impulsion to break loose from the moorings in material reality already attenuated in Locke's philosophy and thrash about in a cloudland of self-enclosed sense-data divorced from the external world. This fatal flaw in their theory of knowledge has made it difficult for the positivists to escape from subjectivity except through an act of "animal faith," *i.e.,* an irrational belief in the existence of the surrounding universe. Or else they have been driven toward semi-idealistic and even solipsistic options.

The immense distance that latter-day empiricism has traveled from its pristine association with materialism can be measured by contrasting the views of Hobbes and Mach. Hobbes defined philosophy as reasoning about causes and effects generated by matter in motion and known through sensation and computation. Mach denied that causation was anything more than a conventional and convenient idea, and he was dubious about the capacity of sensations to reach beyond themselves and convey genuine knowledge of an objective world.

Under social pressures these nonmaterialist trends have become more and more pronounced among twentieth-century empiricists. As capitalism has had to struggle not for supremacy against archaic opponents, but for survival against the ideas and forces of the working-class movement, the adherents of empiricism and positivism have been playing a less and less progressive role. Instead of probing deeper into reality, the positivists have been turning away from it and withdrawing into an increasingly impoverished subjectivism. Instead of reducing and removing barriers to knowledge, they incline to contract its scope and set up bounds to its extension. Baffled by social-historical processes they can neither understand nor control, in their fear and flight they mistake the limitations of their own theorizing and capacities for action for inherent restrictions on human knowledge and social evolution.

7

The obsolescence of empiricism

The once potent empirical viewpoint has been rendered obsolete by mightier developments in many domains of modern life and learning. Its positions have been undermined and its arguments invalidated by advances in the sciences of nature and of society and their implications for philosophic thought. They have become increasingly untenable with revolutionary changes both in the capitalist system and in the relations between its principal classes.

Empiricism first of all broke down in its former stronghold: the theory of knowledge. Since the eighteenth century other schools of Western philosophy have exposed the inconsistencies and inadequacies of the empirical method in the field of epistemology and then proceeded to solve the problems which empiricism as such could not surmount.

Empiricism, rationalism and dialectical materialism

Francis Bacon pointed out in the preface to *The Great Instauration* that what he sought to attain in his work was a "true and lawful marriage between the empirical and rational faculty, the unkind and ill-starred divorce and separation of which has thrown into confusion all the affairs of the human family." The unification of these two faculties is indispensable for any correct theory of knowledge.

Bacon set out to achieve this unification along the empirical road. He gave priority in this marriage to experience, making reason its servant. The founder of British materialism and the progenitor of empiricism indicated the proper path for science and philosophy to pursue.

Empiricism, in the sense that everything we know is founded upon our contacts with external reality through the senses, must be the fundamental starting point for any valid theory of knowledge. As such, it has been integrated into modern materialism, just as it was the keystone of the materialism of Bacon and Hobbes. Dialectical materialism has preserved and developed this valuable acquisition of theoretical investigation and practical experimentation.

Empiricism becomes inadequate and misleading, however, when it elevates sensation into an all-sufficient and self-supporting explanation of knowledge. Sense experience is the basis and beginning of all we know—but it does not constitute nor can it alone account for the whole of knowledge.

"Since everything that comes into the human mind enters through the gates of sense, man's first reason is a reason of sense-experience," wrote Rousseau in *Emile*. This is true. But the mentality which is first formed by sense experience and practical activity based upon it reacts upon its data, reshapes and refines it into ideas. After sensation, as Locke insisted, comes the work of reflection.

Sensations result in the perceptions of things and their interconnections; these in turn give birth to concepts and chains of concepts. The collective historical experience of mankind, based upon its practical activities, produces, along with the necessities of life, generalizations about the nature of things which go beyond crude sensation of particulars. Our capacities and modes of reasoning grow in accord with the development of the forces of production and the social relations these create. The lessons of social experience, the formulated conclusions of practical trials and errors involved in investigation, the results of critical analysis and reflective thought constitute the theoretical content of science. These hypotheses, theories, generalizations are summarized in definite sets of doctrines, groups of tested laws, and rules of procedure proper to each department of knowledge.

This ever growing fund of knowledge is the most precious product of experience. This valid residue of social practice, codified in principles, constitutes the inescapable presupposition of all further experience and serves as its guide.

The rationalists were the principal competitor of the empiricists in the heyday of bourgeois thought. They contested the one-sided approach of the empirical school, which emphasized the origin and content of knowledge while slighting its characteristic and historically developing forms. The idealists stressed the active role of the rational faculty in the generation of knowledge and the necessary part its forms played in ordering the raw materials of sense experience.

For a long time in the bourgeois epoch, philosophy swung helplessly back and forth between these polar opposites. The rival schools kept asking themselves and challenging each other: Was sensory experience or generalizing reason the decisive ingredient in making knowledge? The empiricists from Locke to Mill hinged their positions on the evidence and claims of experience; the rationalists from Descartes to Hegel, on logical demonstration and the alleged "clear and evident" ideas of reason.

Hume had exposed the fundamental flaw in pure empiricism as an adequate explanation of knowledge when he pointed out that the generality and necessity of the categories of thought required for a scientific explanation of reality were not immediately evident in sense experience. Where, then, did the belief in such universal and necessary relations as causality come from? Hume answered that such beliefs were the outcome of logical inference and psychological association. Although required for human action, they had no anchorage in objective reality.

Hume thereby sharpened the problem that awoke Kant from "his dogmatic slumbers," namely, what were the connections between the categories of thought and the data of sensation which guaranteed universal and necessary validity to the results of reasoning? Kant agreed with Hume that time, space and causality could not be accounted for through sense experience alone; on the other hand, he declared, against the idealists, that what these categories organized could not be independent of such experience. Kant tried to overcome the opposition between the universal categories of reason and the particular content of sense experience with the formula that concepts without percepts (empirical sensory content) are empty; percepts without concepts are blind.

His contentions that knowledge had a complex and compound constitution and that both sensibility and understanding were essential for scientific knowledge were correct. But Kant's solution to the problem of the relations between percepts and concepts did not avoid the pitfalls of his predecessors. Neither the forms of intuition (space and time) nor the twelve basic categories of thought in his system were for him derived from sense experience.

These were present in us from the beginning as frames for arranging the material of sensation. But it remained a mystery how and from what source men acquired these particular frames, and not others, in ordering the content of experience in the first place.

Although Kant started with the attempt to validate empirical knowledge, he landed in the idealist heaven of a priori notions. In trying to go beyond Hume, Kant actually fell behind Locke who denied all innate ideas.

Hegel came much closer to solving the problem by pointing out that experience and reason were both essential factors in a rounded theory of knowledge, just as empiricism and abstract rationalism were both necessary, though one-sided, phases in the development of modern philosophy. He asserted that sensation, perception, conception and logical thought were successively different ways of grasping the same essential content of experience and probing ever more deeply into reality. Each had its place and function in the ceaseless and ever deepening process of knowledge.

Although Hegel held fast to the organic connection between sense experience and reason, he went wrong in making an ultimate result of human activity, thought processes and their ideas, the primary factor of reality. He reversed the real relations between material things and their reflections in the mind, between the objective and subjective aspects of experience. The categories of thought are mental reproductions of physical and social realities. The substance of knowledge is taken from the external environment but its special forms are the product of conceptual determinations which are socially and historically conditioned.

Such a definitive solution to the problem of the relations between experience and reason was given by dialectical materialism. The Marxist theory of knowledge accepted the principal affirmations of both schools—the empirical contention that all the contents of knowledge are derived from sense experience and the rationalist counterclaim that its forms were provided by the understanding. But it did not take over either of these propositions in their sweeping and oversimplified original versions.

Marxism subjected both principles to a critical reexamination which led to their reintegration into a new synthesis. Experience and reason were viewed as correlative elements of concrete social practice, determined and shaped by the productive activities of mankind. The concept of experience held by the traditional empiricists was stripped of its unhistorical, abstract, and individualistic traits. It was reinterpreted as the outcome of the action of nature upon mankind and the ever more powerful reaction of toiling mankind upon nature in the progress of social life. Human experience was no longer regarded as a fixed but as a historically developing whole which had changed its contents and diversified its forms with the advancement of technique, science, and culture.

Reason, too, was deprived of any absolute sovereignty over reality, of its formalism and its static attributes. It was equated to the evolving mental capacities of mankind. These have been progressing from the first glimmers of insight provided by the primitive mentality to increasing knowledge of the world as the productive powers of society grew and human control over the operations of nature and society was enlarged.

Thus the two factors, each of which had been the basis for independent and antagonistic philosophies, were transformed into interrelated aspects of a single process. They became the twin poles of the active, productive, feeling, thinking individual, historically emerging out of the social practice of humanity as it engaged in the reconstruction of the natural and social environments.

In the production and reproduction of human life, these interpenetrating opposites acted and reacted upon each other in a ceaseless continuum of development. Experience gave birth to reflection whose results fructified and directed further experience. This conceptually enriched experience in turn corrected, tested, and amplified the results of reasoning—and so on, in a never ending spiral.

The decline of the mechanical world-view

The empirical philosophy not only became outmoded in the theory of knowledge where it claimed to be strongest. Its underpinnings were weakened and removed by further developments in the natural sciences.

1) Defects of mechanical thinking

Empiricism, as has been noted, was the most characteristic philosophical correlative of the mechanical conception of the world. The mechanical system, and its associated methods of thought, held sway in the field of natural science for 250 years. Under its guidance, knowledge of the physical world and control over its processes registered tremendous triumphs.

Although the mechanical outlook and its attendant metaphysical mode of thought powerfully promoted the investigation of nature and the progress of both the physical and social sciences, it had ineradicable imperfections which were gradually brought to light.

First of all, its approach to things was unhistorical and nonevolutionary. The mechanical-minded thinkers disregarded two of the most fundamental features of reality: its never ending change and its constant production of novelty. For them, the fundamental framework of nature was essentially fixed and final. Bodies in motion repeated their predetermined courses forever, and nothing really new issued from them.

This changelessness was most evident in their astrophysics. Once God had created the universe, it stayed as it was. The planets revolved in their appointed orbits; the earth turned but it did not change; the fauna and flora on its surface were no less fixed in their species.

Human nature likewise remained substantially unaltered through the ages. Thus Hobbes in his *Philosophical Rudiments concerning Government and Society* said that he "treated men, not as products of historical development, but as if but now sprung out of the earth and suddenly, like mushrooms, come to full maturity." Hume wrote in his essay on Liberty and Necessity in the *Enquiry:* "There is great uniformity among the actions of men, in all nations and ages, and human nature remains still the same, in its principles and operations . . . Mankind are so much the same, in all times and places, that history informs us of nothing new or strange in this particular."

Nature, society, and the human mind were all governed by unvarying laws which reflected the uniform action of self-identical phenomena.

Their denial of the differences resulting from real development led the mechanists to blank out the many qualitatively distinct modes of motion in the world. They restricted the mode of change in nature to a single fundamental form, the displacement of bodies from one space to another in a given period of time under the impact of external forces. This purely mechanical action was the sole manifestation of matter; all other types of movement and activity were reduced, or reducible, to this one alone.

This pinched definition of motion was coupled with the conception that matter had no inner source of movement but was inherently inert. These correlated notions opened the doors to God. If matter was not self-active, motion had to be introduced into the world from some other source. So God started the machinery of the cosmos he created, though it continued to run thereafter by means of external forces acting on its parts.

In addition, the diverse aspects and energies which are unified and interactive within nature were treated as though they were isolated from one another. They were frozen into absolutely separate entities. Thus Newton took the basic categories of his world-view, time, space, mass, and motion, as fixed elements which were qualitatively independent of one another. And then he singled out one physical force—mechanical energy—and made it sovereign over the rest.

In the mechanical system, motion was conserved from one event to another but not converted from one form into another. The conversion of mechanical motion into heat and heat into mechanical motion was looked upon solely from the standpoint of its quantitative properties. In general, quantity was exalted over quality. The qualitative differences in the modes of manifestation of radiant energy were of no account.

Finally, the mechanical school had a rigid conception of determination and an extremely one-sided notion of causation. In the introduction to his *Principia* Newton declared that "it would be desirable to deduce from the elements of mechanics the remaining phenomena of nature." This laid down the main lines of the program of work for natural scientists until well into the nineteenth century.

Laplace claimed that such a goal was at least theoretically in sight. He maintained that a universal intelligence, which knew all the forces of nature and the structure of the beings in it, could analyze them and encompass the movements of the greatest bodies and the lightest particles into a single formula so that nothing would be uncertain and the future and the past would be present before its eyes. Laplace believed that humanity was headed toward such an all-embracing grasp of reality, although it would always be infinitely distant from it.

This mechanistic determinism was based upon the assumption that all the data governing the constitution and operation of things could be given at a single moment and, once these were known, the further course of events contained no novelties and presented no uncertainties. Indeterminism was ruled out as an effective aspect of reality; it was simply the product of man's ignorance.

Just as mechanical action was the sole form of motion and rigid determinism the sole regulator of nature, so the cause completely determined the effect. The effect was not a necessary condition of the cause and capable of reacting upon it. It was a passive result. This oversimplified, one-way conception of causation, which ignored the essential reciprocity of causal relations, could not cope with intricate processes of development.

2) Downfall of mechanical synthesis in physical science

The basic premises of the mechanical world-view were gradually undermined by the spread of the evolutionary outlook through the sciences. Ironically, this new approach was initiated in astronomical theory during the eighteenth century by Laplace himself who, with Kant, advanced the nebular hypothesis of the origin of the solar system. A celestial object was treated not as a changeless fixture, but as the outcome of purely physical processes of formation. In the next century this line of evolutionary reasoning was extended to geology by Lyell and others, and then to organic existence by Darwin and his contemporaries.

As the conception of evolution took hold of one branch of science after another, the mechanical habit of approaching phenomena as immutable entities gave way to the procedure of viewing all things as in ceaseless change and as products of historical development through successive stages of being and becoming.

Meanwhile, the growth of important new departments of scientific knowledge from chemistry to electromagnetism deposed mechanics from its central and commanding place in the assemblage of the sciences. This culminated in the twentieth-century revolution in physics, which laid bare the limitations of Newtonian mechanics and overturned the Laplacean projection of an unrestricted universal determinism which had no room for chance.

The breakdown of mechanistic physics took place during a period of revolution in technology, when mechanical processes were supplemented and then supplanted by non-mechanical ones of an electrical, chemical, or magnetic character. As mechanism yielded its predominance in the technology that moved and changed society and nature, so it lost preeminence in the highest generalizations of philosophical thought about them.

The first step in this direction was taken in the nineteenth century when the steam engine spurred the study of thermodynamics and the problems connected with the conversion of heat into mechanical motion. This brought new aspects of the movement of matter into the spotlight.

The natural scientists of the Newtonian epoch were preoccupied with investigating the laws of movement of separate bodies and molar masses and interpreting these in a mechanical manner. While mechanics deals with that form of motion which consists in the passage of bodies through space, thermodynamics deals with that form of action by which heat is changed into mechanical energy.

Thermodynamics brought forward for consideration, not simply the *transference* of motion from one object to another, but the more complex problem of how one mode of motion (heat) was *transformed* into another (mechanical movement).

In addition to this qualitative change, the problem also had its quantitative side. Was energy lost or conserved, and in what respects and to what degrees, when the transition from one mode of motion to the other was effected? Mayer and Helmholtz demonstrated that energy remained constant during the transformation.

Electromagnetism even more radically upset the classical conceptions. According to Newton's school, bodies occupied a definite region in space. But Maxwell's theory, confirmed by more and more experimental evidence, stated that electricity and magnetism were continuously distributed throughout a field. Unlike an isolated object strictly situated in an independent space, the charged body and its field reciprocally determined each other and were really inseparable.

According to the Newtonian conception, each body has definite properties which can be added to but not fundamentally altered. However, according to the molecular theory of heat and the kinetic theory of gases, materials in the mass can acquire properties which they do not possess singly. There is abundant evidence that a large enough aggregation of internally unaffected bodies can give rise to new qualities.

In classical terms light had either to be a wave or a particle; it could not be—or behave like—both. But experiment disclosed that light exhibits both wavelike and particulate features. This wave-particle duality was later extended through wave mechanics to the structure and behavior of molecules, atoms, and nuclei.

According to the Newtonian scheme, motion was continuous. The quantum theory showed, on the contrary, that molecular and atomic phenomena were discontinuous.

For Newton, time and space were each absolute and independent. The theory of relativity fused the two into a single space-time continuum and made them relative to a specific frame of physical reference.

The previously independent entities of energy and mass were demonstrated, first in theory, then in practice, to be identical. Mass is energy and energy has mass so that under the proper conditions one can be equivalently converted into the other.

The chemical elements, too, which were considered to be independent, irreducible, and unchangeable, have been found to be interlinked, subject to disintegration and to both natural and artificial transmutation. Even the atoms of their molecular structures can be split and fused.

These and similar developments and discoveries produced a crisis in physical theory which has provoked considerable controversy and is yet to be definitively resolved. One thing at least is undeniable. The classical mechanical scheme has manifestly become untenable and must be reconstructed and replaced. That has become a central task of contemporary scientific thought.

Certain consequences logically flow from a recognition of the inadequacies of the old ideas in natural science.

a) Like Euclidean geometry and Aristotelean logic, Newtonian mechanics has a restricted scope and application. It gives an approximate account of certain physical phenomena and has a limited, relative validity. It holds good for low energies, limited distances, long durations.

But where very high energies, extremely short distances, and flashes of time are involved, other concepts, methods, and laws are operative and must be invoked.

b) The exact localization of particles in time and space is a static idealization. This is useful for certain purposes but discounts and disregards the dynamic interrelations, interchanges, and interactions of events.

c) Absolute discontinuity, isolation, and separation in phenomena do not correspond to objective reality. In every natural event one form of energy (radiant, electrical, chemical, mechanical) is being converted into another, always at some well-defined rate of exchange. There is a continuous transformation, as well as conservation, of mass and energy. No one event can be taken in total isolation from others; no one form of motion is primary or predominant under all circumstances. Elements are interconnected and transformable.

d) The levels of being are not only interlinked, interactive, and interconvertible but they are inexhaustible. There is no limit or end to human penetration deeper and deeper into reality and to further knowledge of its processes.

e) Statistical regularities and the laws of chance show that accident and necessity, contingency and determinism, are not mutually exclusive but inseparable and interdependent aspects of the universe which can be transformed into each other.

Such theoretical conclusions from the findings of the natural scientists over the past century are thoroughly compatible with a dialectical and materialist philosophy and were indeed anticipated in principle by its positions. But the confirmation of the changeability and interconnection of everything in the universe and our experience of it has removed the principal props from the mechanical scheme of things. Any empiricism which is rooted in the particularism of objects, relations, and ideas, in the severance of quantity from quality, in the absolute opposition of determinism to indeterminism, and in the immutability of distinct formations, is outmoded.

Empiricism and the evolution of capitalism

Empiricism was superannuated not simply by advances in philosophy and the physical sciences, but by the profound changes in the situation of the bourgeoisie and the prospects of capitalism brought about by the challenge of a revolutionary working-class movement. Neither the upper nor the lower strata of the bourgeoisie have felt the need for a theoretical method which went further than empiricism, rationalism, spiritualism, or idealism.

This conservatism was strongest in the Anglo-American world where, with the consolidation of the capitalist order, empiricism was consecrated as the predominant philosophy. For several centuries it has enjoyed a virtual monopoly of progressive thought in most fields of intellectual endeavor, as well as in everyday life. Capitalism among the English-speaking peoples has evolved up to its monopolist stage without any replacement for the type of thought which presided over its origins. Immense innovations in other departments of the activity of bourgeois society have been combined with an immobility in philosophy which persists to the present day. This is one of the most acute, though scarcely recognized, contradictions in Anglo-American culture.

A renovation of philosophy was called for, among other things, by the entry of the industrial working class as a new revolutionary agency into modern history. This breakthrough was made in the second half of the nineteenth century when the German thinkers, Marx and Engels, worked out the principles of dialectical materialism as the world outlook of the proletarian movement. Their highly original synthesis of revolutionary theory and practice lifted materialist philosophy to unparalleled heights and opened a new epoch in world thought.

Materialism fused with dialectical logic eliminated the mechanical, metaphysical, atomistic, and antihistorical features common to the empiricists and earlier materialist schools. Marxism viewed nature as an independent, unified, infinite complex of material processes governed by laws which developed endlessly in dialectical ways. Every natural, social, and intellectual formation was a transitory product of given material conditions, and it was subject to change, eventual destruction, and replacement through the operation of the conflicting forces at work within itself.

Human history was regarded not as the mechanical repetition of identical factors in differing combinations, but as a genuinely progressive process. Beginning with the emergence of the hominids from the primate stage, mankind has moved ahead through an interlinked evolutionary series of more productive socioeconomic formations. Each of these stages has displayed novel institutions and traits and possessed its own specific laws.

The social structure was not an aggregate of unrelated individuals but an integrated labor collective struggling with nature, whose members were shaped by the prevailing conditions of life and labor.

The state was not an eternal or irremovable institution nor the result of a compact arrived at by the free choice of deliberating individuals. It was the inevitable political outgrowth of class divisions and conflicts instituted in civilized societies by possessing classes. Their rulership was enforced to ensure their domination over the dispossessed working masses, maintain the mode of their exploitation, and assure control over the surplus social product.

Capitalism itself is viewed not as the ultimate form of social existence but as the last link in the chain of class-divided economic systems. In the working class it has organized the antagonistic and creative social force which will be driven to abolish the causes of its miseries by collective revolutionary action and consciously establish a higher social order.

This revolutionary socialist movement could not be satisfied with the same instruments of thought that the bourgeois revolutions so successfully deployed against medieval scholasticism and other antiquated doctrines. The emaciated positivism of middle-class liberalism was even less suitable for the effective execution of the new historical tasks than had been the robust empiricism of the radical bourgeoisie.

Marxism alone provided the finer tools and modern techniques of theory required by the far-reaching objectives of the working-class struggle for emancipation. It quickly became the most formidable rival and predestined replacement for all those ideas which were out of step with the demands of the era of transition from capitalism to socialism.

The qualitatively different needs, interests, and aims of the working-class movement therefore brought into being not only a new force for social transformation, but a new way of analyzing and interpreting reality. Its forms of consciousness and basic categories transcended the limitations of earlier schools of thought.

Marxism did not disdainfully reject empiricism as all wrong, as a mere delusion. It examined empiricism with the same criteria as it did all other precursors in philosophy, carefully and critically sifting its inventory so that true ideas could be discriminated from the false and integrated into the structure of dialectical materialism.

Just as the ablest representatives of the rising bourgeoisie, from Locke to Hegel, had fashioned philosophies with all the resources of knowledge at their disposal, so did the scientific theorists of the working class. However, the upholders of capitalism refuse to believe that representatives of the outlook of the working masses could perform the same high functions as the ideologists of the more privileged, and presumably more intelligent and wiser, classes. How could such partisans be capable of initiating and perfecting a superior philosophy? This is one social source of the widespread disparagement of Marxism and the denial of its claims to provide a higher mode of thought.

The decline and dispossession of empiricism in one field after another is not a haphazard but a lawful phenomenon. It is an integral part of the vast historical process of the disintegration of capitalist civilization and culture on a world scale and its replacement by forces creative of the socialist future. This is the only correct way of viewing the issues at stake in the confrontation between empiricism and Marxism.

Experience has shown that the process of intellectual modernization, by which dialectical materialism supersedes the diverse forms of bourgeois thought, develops extremely unevenly from country to country and from one sphere of social life to another. General ideas change much slower than other social factors. Despite its superiorities, the Marxist method and its conceptions have far from dislodged empirical habits of thought, even in many parts of the socialist and labor movement. These cannot be uprooted without a stubborn and prolonged struggle on the key problems of philosophical thought and scientific procedure, as we propose to show in the next chapters.

8

Habits of empirical thought

Empirical philosophy and its evolution may interest scholars, but, it may be asked, what use is this history to a worker in the socialist ranks? Why should he be concerned with a criticism of empirical habits of thought?

First of all, for practical reasons. Although the philosophy of empiricism is as antiquated as the candle, its ideas and methods persist and do considerable harm to the cause of labor. The current influence of empiricism upon the organizations of the working class gives immediate point and political purpose to a study of its characteristics.

The empirical approach to problems is rooted in the conditions of everyday life in bourgeois society and in its education. The bad habits of thought thus nurtured are reinforced by the policies and outlook of the labor leaderships. Empiricism is the guiding line of the union officialdom, who are content to live from day to day, from one contract to the next, and from one craft and sectional division to another. They do not act with any clear and unified conception of labor's social role or of the historical objectives of the union movement.

The right-wing Labour Party leaders in England have the same attitude of "muddling through" from election to election and from one national and international emergency to another. They rely upon improvisations and impressions on how to snare the elusive "floating vote" rather than upon a worked-out long-range program based upon the revolutionary mission of the working class.

This traditional mode of thought has been eulogized as "peculiarly" British by one of its foremost adepts, Lord Attlee. In his autobiography he wrote: "It has always been our practice, in accord with the natural genius of the British people, to work empirically. We were not afraid of compromises and partial solutions. We knew that mistakes would be made and that advance would often be by trial and error. We realized that the application of socialist principles in a country such as Britain, with a peculiar economic structure based on international trade, required great flexibility." (*As It Happened,* p. 229)

There in a nutshell is the ex-Prime Minister's reasoned explanation, or rather apology, for the fatal shortcomings of his Labour administrations. If nationalizations of key industries were so costly, limited, and bureaucratic, if the House of Lords was allowed to remain, if certain colonial possessions were relinquished so slowly and only because of irresistible pressures, if the Atlantic Alliance with U.S. imperialism against the workers' states was cemented, etc.—"we were not afraid of compromise and partial solutions," this bold reformist proclaims.

The workers might well say to Attlee and his successors: "Please, next time you take over the government, do not be so ready to compromise at *our* expense. If you must proceed by trial and error, why not try revolutionary methods at the expense of the capitalists for a change? You might promote the cause of socialism better and avoid so many errors."

However, Harold Wilson, the Labour Party's Prime Minister of the nineteen-sixties, has not only followed in Attlee's footsteps but has outdone his pragmatic predecessor in striving to salvage a sinking national capitalism at the sacrifice of socialist principles and at the expense of the welfare of the working people.

Although empiricism is native to Britain, it has not been confined to that island. Ever since the turn of the century, when Eduard Bernstein explicitly rejected the dialectical materialism of Marx and Engels in favor of empiricism, this creed has been the dominant mode of thought among the revisionists of Marxism and the reformist heads of the Social-Democracy. It has become the philosophy of opportunism, of impermissible concessions to reaction, and eventually of craven surrender to capitalist pressures. That is why its real nature and current functions in politics should be grasped by every worker.

In a memorable polemic on this very subject, conducted in the last year of his life, Trotsky wrote: "The question of a correct philosophical doctrine, that is, a correct method of thought, is of decisive significance to a revolutionary party just as a good machine shop is of decisive significance to production. It is still possible to defend the old society with the material and intellectual methods inherited from the past. It is absolutely unthinkable that this old society can be overthrown and a new one constructed without first critically analyzing the current methods." (*In Defense of Marxism,* p. 151)

The strengths and weaknesses of empiricism

Empiricism has many virtues. Its reliance upon direct observation and the results of experiment, its closeness to practice, its preference for the facts, even at times its distrust of far-flown abstractions in favor of sturdy commonsense judgment, are useful and necessary qualities.

In exceptional cases pure empiricism has risen to the heights of genius among Englishmen. The twin peaks of achievement in nineteenth-century natural science are identified with Faraday and Darwin. That great pioneer in experimental research, Faraday, did not arrive at his epoch-making generalizations in physics through any deliberated method, although his conclusions were highly dialectical. He discovered electromagnetic induction and developed his concept of the electromagnetic field by means of an empirical "hunch" that the various powers of nature he was familiar with, chemical affinity, heat, electricity, magnetism, and gravitation, were all interlinked, interconvertible, and came from a common source.

"Now consider a little more generally the relation of all these powers," he wrote in 1834. "We cannot say that any one is the cause of the others, but only that all are connected and due to one common cause. As to the connection, observe the productions of any one from another, or the conversion of one into another."

Fifteen years later, in 1849, Faraday wrote again: "The exertions in physical science of late years have been directed to ascertain not merely the natural powers, but the manner in which they are linked together, the universality of each one in its action, and their probable *unity in one*."

Faraday's need for direct personal observation of phenomena was so strong that this empirical-minded scientist could not be satisfied with the results of other people's experiments. "I was never able to make a fact my own without seeing it," he wrote to a friend in 1860, "and the descriptions of the best works altogether failed to convey to my mind, such a knowledge of things as to allow myself to form a judgment upon them. If Grove, or Wheatstone, or Gassiot, or any other told me a new fact and wanted my opinion, either of its value, or the cause, or the evidence it would give in any subject, I never could say anything until I had seen the fact."

During this same period Darwin was examining the causes of evolution of living organisms and developing dialectical generalizations of a comparably high order in the same empirical way. In an autobiographical sketch Darwin stated that, in starting his enquiry, he "worked on true Baconian principles, and, without any theory, collected facts on a wholesale scale."

The exceptional powers of insight vested in a Faraday and Darwin compensated for the handicaps of an inferior philosophy. But such gifted individuals do not come along every day. The rest of mankind can get better results by using a more efficient method which does not work on hunches or collect facts "without any theory." Intuitions are erratic and facts without the illumination of a correct theory are opaque. The defects of empiricism set traps for unwary and inexperienced people.

Empiricism instills and encourages many harmful habits of thought. Chief among these are inconclusiveness, relativism, impressionism, eclecticism, subjectivism, and skepticism. These tendencies have been present to one degree or another in the principal exponents of this school on the main problems of philosophy. They are likewise characteristic of its practitioners in many fields of activity.

The curse of indecision

Inconclusiveness was implanted in the original foundations of empiricism, as has been explained, because its advocates failed to take a firm stand on such basic issues of philosophy as the relation between ideas (sense impressions) and objective reality, and on the nature of reality itself. This indecisiveness in fundamental theory has been extended by empiricists into other spheres of knowledge and activity.

At times this has culminated in pure relativism. William James, the American pragmatist, asked in his last published essay: "What is concluded that we might conclude in regard to it?" Where does such an extremely unassertive assertion spring from? It comes from the presupposition that reality is so indeterminate and our knowledge of its features so uncertain that nothing can be positively stated and definitely maintained. The pragmatic significance of this philosophical relativism is the injunction to refrain from taking definite positions on disputed issues, making lasting commitments to the contending sides, or sticking to any conclusions arrived at.

In politics such a theoretical outlook is very congenial to habitual waverers on fundamental issues. For example, let the question be posed point-blank to Mr. In-Between: "Is capitalism an utterly reactionary, decrepit, and doomed system which is destined to be replaced by the more progressive system of socialism?" The answer of a convinced militant of Marxism is "Yes," and he will work steadfastly to assure the victory of the socialist forces over capitalism.

The empiricist, however, will try to avoid giving a categorical "yes" or "no" answer to this question. His usual pretext is: The present structure of society and the tendencies of its development are as yet too uncertain for us to tell in advance; other alternatives may be open, so "let us wait and see." Such a theoretical outlook paralyzes revolutionary action.

Even after the inveterate empiricist embraces the socialist cause in words, he is still confronted with the problem of how to implement it in practice. Let him be asked to choose between the methods of class collaboration and class struggle, and he will be inclined to reason: It cannot be determined beforehand which of these opposing ways will best promote the interests of labor. Let us try now this and now that and then see what happens.

Nine times out of ten, however, this abstract impartiality masks a bias for accepting unnecessary compromise in the particular instance. The empiricist opts for the line of *least* resistance since he does not see the political and class necessity for the path of *militant* resistance to the encroachments of capitalist power.

Impressionism and dialectics

The dialectical thinker Hegel was an unsparing critic of empiricism. He condemned it on the ground that it dwelt too much on the sensuous surface of phenomena and did not seek out their underlying essence or penetrate to their driving forces. Empiricism, he said, exalted the incidental at the expense of the necessary and lawful aspects of things and mistook their outward appearances for the inner reality. The inevitable result of such an empirical approach was impressionism.

Rational science aims to take an objectively based view of events in their totality and in their whole course of development and seeks to discover their essential connections and main motive forces. Impressionism relies upon personally enclosed or otherwise narrowed experiences as the practical standard for appraising and analyzing phenomena. Such subjective and superficial views of a situation, made under the impact of immediate circumstances or the influence of external interests, can lead to hasty, inadequate, and misleading conclusions.

Does capitalism, for example, necessarily increase the national wealth and the standard of living? It might be deduced from a narrow inspection of its operations and achievements that it does so, at least in the highly developed industrialized countries. Such, in fact, is the claim of its apologists.

But if capitalism is looked at in its entirety, from the inner structure of its social relations to the dynamics of its development, the reality differs from the episodic appearances. Increased productivity and improved living standards are not the fundamental aims of capitalism; they are accessory aspects and impermanent consequences of its operations. The primary, constant, and essential drive of the system is the production of surplus value for the owners of the means of production. When the economy or any part of it cannot function at a profit, production slows down or is halted, regardless of the effects on the national wealth or the people's welfare.

Moreover, whereas capitalism in its progressive stages expanded the productive forces of society more than any other economic system, in its present imperialist death agony it curbs, chokes, and destroys them. The impressionist who believes in the innate beneficence of capitalism therefore bases his judgment upon a partial picture of the system and a short-range snapshot of its life-span.

Evolution and revolution in English history

Popular as it is, this impressionistic method of thought is equally unreliable as a guide to understanding the complex modes of development in history. Must fundamental social change come about through revolutionary class action and political upheavals, as Marxism contends, or does it proceed by way of class accommodation? Let us select

England for a case study.

Conservatives, Liberals, and right-wing Labourites point to English experience since 1688 and triumphantly conclude: "Class conflicts do arise but the English way, sir, is to settle them by compromise." This protects the property of the plutocrats and their peace of mind at one and the same time.

It is not easy to refute such a conclusion if one's view is restricted to that single segment of English history, taken in isolation from everything else. The fact is that, despite sporadic revolutionary impulses and actions, there has not been any successful social or political revolution in Colonel Blimp's island since 1688.

But wait a moment, reply the Marxists. What about the preceding events from the sixteen-forties to the sixteen-eighties? Don't the civil wars of that crucial century belong to English history, too? And don't they have to be taken into account? Isn't revolution to be included along with gradualism in the English way?

If the two periods from 1640 to 1690 and from 1690 to the present are considered independently of each other, the historical experience of England since the rise of capitalism appears to offer no single categorical solution to the dispute. Or rather, it offers two contradictory answers. Sometimes the struggle of social forces proceeds in an evolutionary manner; at another time by way of revolution. The one conclusion cancels out the other, and we might well repeat after William James: "What is concluded that we might conclude in regard to it?"

However, the matter is not quite so hopeless. At this point a dialectical approach, which enjoins us to see things in their interconnections and transmutations, can come to our rescue. For it is wrong to judge these contrasting periods apart from each other. They have to be studied scientifically in their organic association as consecutive phases of a unified process of bourgeois-democratic development.

The civil wars of the seventeenth century created the indispensable foundations for the political rule of the bourgeoisie and the subsequent growth and diversification of British capitalism. The primary, essential, necessary preconditions for the flourishing of several centuries of gradualism were laid down in the few convulsive decades of revolution. Those empirical-minded politicians who locate the core of English history in its gradualism do so by severing the luxuriant reforms of the eighteenth and nineteenth centuries from their revolutionary roots in the seventeenth century.

That is not all. The historical framework has to be widened still further. It is not enough to grasp the links between the bourgeois social and political revolutions of the seventeenth century and the capitalist evolution of the eighteenth and nineteenth centuries. It is also necessary to see the connections between the insular experiences of the English people and the international setting within which they actually unfolded.

Only then will it become evident that later revolutionary events in America and on the European continent spurred the granting of reforms by the ruling classes within England itself and that the material means for making these concessions possible came from Britain's monopoly of the world market and its colonial dominions. Victorious wars, colonial plunder, and revolutions abroad were equally vital ingredients in the prolonged stability of British capitalist rule and its domestic policy of doled-out reforms. The bourgeoisie avoided violent upheavals and assured peaceful development within its own borders only by benefiting from the violent changes it introduced into the lives of other peoples.

So much for the past. What about the future? What are the prospects for England in the last third of the twentieth century? Will there be a continuation of the class compromises of the immediate past or an outbreak on a higher historical level of class conflicts as intense as those of the mid-seventeenth century?

Whatever the impressionists say or the empiricists do, the conditions are ripening both within England and outside it not for the indefinite maintenance of the old relations and policies, but for a new phase of revolutionary advancement. The transfer of Britain's supremacy to the United States, the loss of her colonial tributaries, the growing strength of the postcapitalist countries, and the shakiness of England's economy are preparing new and heightened clashes between imperialist conservatism and the labor movement.

The pattern of events in store will resemble those of the Cromwellian years much more than those of Victoria's reign, because at stake once again is the abolition of an ancient order, the passage of supremacy from an enfeebled ruling class to an irresistible new one, and the rebuilding of the economy on higher foundations. This time it is not the feudal structure that has to be replaced by a capitalist one, but an imperialist regime by a workers' government heading toward socialism.

It is this dialectical reversal of the previous trends in English history that will have to be thought out by the coming revolutionary leaders of labor and fought out by the working class itself.

Empiricism and common sense

Such a radical conclusion may be repugnant to that shortsighted common sense which guides the average citizen in everyday affairs. The content of common sense is a hodgepodge of elementary conclusions from experience combined with prejudices derived from past conditions and from ideas restricted to the framework of ordinary life in bourgeois society. These are frozen into hard-and-fast conceptions on the tacit assumption that the conditions which produced and sustained these commonplaces will persist indefinitely without drastic change.

Each stratum of bourgeois society mingles its own special prejudices with the more general commonsense conceptions. The policies of the Conservative statesmen during the Suez misadventure show how disastrous such thinking, which operates with fixed notions based on short-range views, can be even on the ruling-class level.

Prime Minister Eden acted in 1956 as though the conditions that brought success to British foreign policy in 1856 were still in force. He discounted the sweeping historical changes which make the lesser Elizabeth's reign so different from that of Queen Victoria.

The colonial peoples are now in irresistible revolt. The old dominions, from Canada to India, can no longer be pushed around like pawns by London; they have independent status. England has become a second-rate factor in world economic, diplomatic, and military affairs. It must yield, however grudgingly, to the United States on the one side and to the Soviet Union on the other. This once majestic power has become a satellite of American imperialism with little room for maneuver on its own account. Its degradation is an expression of the decline of the imperialist system on a world-historical scale.

Finally, British labor has grown to such stature and become so conscious a political force that, even under right-wing auspices, it can exercise some veto power over the direction of Tory foreign policy. The effect of the massive Trafalgar Square demonstration called by the Labour

Party to protest the Suez aggression against Egypt in 1956 testified to this.

The poor "common sense" of the Conservatives proved helpless to cope with this reversal in Britain's world position. The Tory warriors of 1956, animated by ideas proper to the days of Palmerston, appeared as ridiculous as Don Quixote who conducted himself by feudal standards after medieval conditions had passed away.

In general, the conclusions of common sense remain valid only to the extent that the conditions which bred them remain essentially unaltered. The Tories suffered shipwreck in the Suez crisis because they failed to recognize the contradiction between Britain's past and present roles on the world arena. In this epoch, long-standing international relations are being upset by the clashes of mighty social forces; many former landmarks are being swept away. Under such revolutionary circumstances the once trustworthy commonplaces that the British Foreign Office steered by have not only become unreliable but positively harmful even to their Conservative sponsors.

Logical positivism: The degradation of empirical philosophy

The empiricism which is so characteristic of English thinking exists nowadays in widely different forms and places. If it flourishes on the practical level as homely "common sense," it survives at the other extreme in the highly abstract propositions of logical positivism, linguistic analysis, and kindred philosophical theories taught by university professors who say they have no application to practical life.

The impoverishment of empiricism is no less flagrant in the more restricted province of contemporary philosophy than it is in the more familiar field of imperialist policy.

The most advanced symptoms of its debility can be seen in logical positivism. This is a belated offspring of English empiricism born in Austria after the first world war and reared in English and American universities where it found sanctuary.

Logical positivism, especially in the form of linguistic analysis, resembles classical British empiricism as a senile and impotent pedant resembles a lusty iconoclastic youth. Locke, the founder of empiricism, was confident that, despite the limitations on our knowledge, the human understanding could know the external world and deal effectively with it. The logical positivists question whether the mind can give us any certain knowledge of the real world; some even doubt whether such a world can be demonstrated to exist.

Locke analyzed, among other things, the functions of precise terms in the process of knowledge. But, like Hobbes, he held that "words are wise men's counters; they do but reckon by them; but they are the money of fools." The logical positivists are "foolish" in this sense. They think that words are more important for reasoning than the realities they represent. Instead of focusing upon real things and relations and their conceptual reflections in the human mind, they limit themselves to dissecting the structure of sentences and fussing endlessly and fruitlessly over the multiple meanings of logical formulations and grammatical terms. They envisage philosophy as though it had:

> No belly and no bowels.
> Only consonants and vowels.

It is useful and often necessary to eliminate unclarities and ambiguities from language to improve the functioning of that indispensable instrument of thought. But it is a paltry enterprise to convert this task into the paramount aim of philosophy. On the intellectual plane this is equivalent to reducing the process and purpose of material production to the sharpening and cleaning of a tool.

The problems of philosophy tend to be reduced in their writings to arguments over words and their exact references (semantics). In reviewing the life and work of Ludwig Wittgenstein, the Homer of this school, Gilbert Ryle, Professor of Metaphysical Philosophy at Oxford, remarked: "It comes natural to us to think of both logic and philosophy as concerned not with any ordinary or extraordinary kinds of *things,* but with the meanings of the expressions of our thoughts and knowledge . . ." (*Scientific American,* September, 1957)

What "comes natural" to these professors would have revolted the pioneer empiricists of the seventeenth century. Their theorizing had aims and results very different from those of their twentieth-century descendants. Bacon, Locke, Hume dealt death blows to medieval scholasticism. The logical positivists have created a modern scholasticism which threshes the empty husks of once valuable ideas, and squabbles over the meanings and relations of terms apart from their connections with things in their development.

Locke condemned the "empty, idle" theorizing of the scholastics of his own day and scorned any philosophy that could not be put to practical use in social life or in science. "They that are studiously busy in the cultivating and adorning of such dry barren notions," he wrote, "are vigorously employed to little purpose, and might with as much reason have retrimmed, now they are men, the babies they made when they were children, as exchanged them for these empty impracticable notions which, however dressed up are, after forty years' dandling, but puppets still, void of strength, use and activity."

The logical positivists boast that their inquiries have no traffic with material realities but are concerned solely with clarifying ideas—though they have little success even in that limited purpose. Their "dry barren notions" remain "after forty years' dandling, but puppets still, void of strength, use and activity."

Whereas common sense is the content of popular empiricism, these academic empiricists are contemptuous of the simplest notions of common sense. On the basis of continued experience the average adult believes that an external world exists, that other people have thoughts, feelings, and motives like his own, that it is possible to know the past, and to be certain about some matters.

The logical positivists (who are neither very logical nor very positive) cast doubt on all these common sense propositions. "Such assumptions may be unavoidable in practical life," they argue, "but our critical reason cannot find any logical warrant for believing in their validity."

The unempirical empiricism of A.J. Ayer

The English Marxist Maurice Cornforth has ably criticized the skepticism and subjectivism of such contemporary empiricists as Bertrand Russell, Ludwig Wittgenstein, and Rudolf Carnap in two works of somewhat varying views: *Science versus Idealism* (1955) and *Marxism and the Linguistic Philosophy* (1965). It would duplicate effort to go over the same ground.

Let us turn to a younger exponent of the same line of thought, A.J. Ayer, Grote Professor of Philosophy of Mind and Logic in the University of London. He is not only esteemed as the most brilliant of present-day British empiricists but, as editor of the *Pelican Philosophy Series*, exerts a direct influence on British popular education in philosophy.

In 1956 Professor Ayer published a defense of "Philosophical Skepticism" in *Contemporary British Philosophy, Third Series.* This article, which summarizes views he set forth in earlier works, decants a distillation of the phenomenalism, subjectivism, and skepticism that have marked the academic empiricism of our century. The colorless concoction he serves up in his clear prose contains not a single substantial ingredient to nourish the intellect which craves to know what philosophy has to say about the nature of reality.

Bernard Shaw once wrote a novel called *The Unsocial Socialist.* Professor Ayer's essay might more appropriately have been entitled *The Pseudo-Skeptical Skeptic* or *An Unempirical Empiricist.*

He asks whether any rational grounds can be found for asserting that what is not directly and immediately observable exists. Among such things are the material world, other people's minds, the past, and the future. "It would be a heroic skeptic who maintained that we had no right whatsoever to be sure, or even moderately confident, of anything concerning the existence of physical objects, of the minds of others, or the past," Ayer writes.

Unlike Hume, Ayer is no such heroic skeptic. He neither affirms that such realities may exist nor denies their existence. He merely contends that they cannot be demonstrated to exist on any rational basis. He is a skeptic afraid to accept the consequences of his own skepticism, as an adoring adolescent fears to embrace the embodiment of his affections.

Ayer is an avowed empiricist—and yet he expressly disclaims the elementary principle of empiricism. He asserts that experience cannot be called in to decide between the materialist and the agnostic on the real existence of the external world, because "the subject of their dispute is just how any such experience can be interpreted." He argues: "In general the philosophical skeptic sets out to disqualify the various sources of knowledge. But this disqualification is carried out on a priori grounds. It is independent of the candidate's actual performances."

This reasoning shows how great is the distance separating Locke from Ayer. The seventeenth-century thinker rejected any a priori tests for knowledge and appealed exclusively to the facts of experience—in principle, if not always in practice. His semiskeptical twentieth-century descendant explicitly repudiates experience as the supreme test of truth and reverts to a priori grounds. One can imagine Locke turning over in his grave and moaning: "If this be empiricism, then I at least am no empiricist!"

Professor Ayer goes on to tell us that neither the actual causes nor the practical consequences of any philosophical position can have any bearing on its truth or falsity. Every theoretical statement has to conform to some impossible absolute criteria set up by the skeptic before it can be stamped with the sign of real knowledge. Since no single proposition can pass such arbitrary tests—not even the simple statement that I or the world exist—all knowledge remains suspect.

In the youth of British empiricism, Locke set out to discover the real sources of valid knowledge and found it in experience and reflection. In its old age, Ayer disqualifies experience as the test of real knowledge in favor of a barren "pure reason." Thus, in the course of three centuries British empiricism has become transformed into its opposite, from a theory of relatively certain and useful knowledge into a theory of no certain knowledge.

From the theoretical standpoint this modern empiricism represents the decay and desiccation of a once vigorous and fruitful branch of philosophy. From the social standpoint it indicates how the certainties of the militant bourgeoisie in the prime of capitalist growth have been supplanted by the skeptical laments of learned professors. They hesitate to come to grips with the most crucial issues in philosophy and give definite answers to them just as so many of their fellow middle-class intellectuals resist taking firm stands on the fundamental questions of politics.

The organic eclecticism of empiricism

Empiricism resists systematization because of the lack of coherence in its fundamental ideas and the coexistence within it of incompatible tendencies and contrary principles. For the very same reason, as a blend of materialist and idealist views mixed in varying proportions from one empiricist to another and from one period of its development to the next, empiricism is organically eclectic. It lends itself to the most unstable combinations in theory and practice.

British politicians of all shades from the Tories to the right-wing Labourites have an international reputation for subordinating their principles to temporarily advantageous expedients. Labour Party leaders countenance policies and commit actions which violate the principles of democracy, not to speak of the ideas of socialism on which they presumably stand. They become lords. They don knee breeches and kowtow before the monarch. They tolerate a state-established church. And they have few qualms in reconciling obeisance to these feudal anachronisms with their socialist convictions. Some even defend such support with phony arguments.

Their conception of "the mixed economy" in the capitalist welfare state is an outstanding example of their deep-seated eclecticism. It is one of the cardinal truths of socialism, recognized in the original Labour Party program, that without the abolition of capitalist proprietorship and profit the material means for building a new society remain beyond the control of the working class. Centralized public ownership of the principal means of production and exchange, democratically controlled and operated by the working people, is the prime necessity for a planned and progressively expanding economy.

The new Fabian advocates of the welfare state fling aside this elementary socialist principle and praise the merits of private ownership of certain key industries alongside government management of others. The coexistence of two such antagonistic sectors produces better results, they contend, than would any monopoly of ownership and unified administration of the nation's economy by a workers' regime.

The reformists justify the inconsistency of their economic theory with the socialist program on the ground that it will produce better results. But the difficulties into which the Fabianized capitalism of Great Britain is heading demonstrates that these eclectics are not only unsocialist in theory but equally wrong in regard to the benefits obtainable in practice from their lauded "mixed-up" economy.

In A.D. 616, during the transition from tribal to Christian times in Britain, Redewold, King of the East Anglicans, erected a temple in which was placed one altar to Christ and another for sacrifices to pagan gods. The Labour leaders today behave like this ancient king. They have come over to socialism—without discarding bourgeois values and ideas. They embrace bourgeois parliamentarism and workers' power, private enterprise and public ownership. And the incongruity of worshiping both at the same time is not even apparent to them.

Subjectivism and skepticism

Since Bishop Berkeley set forth his subjective idealism and Hume his doubts about any rational proofs for the objective existence of causation and natural law, subjectivism and skepticism have tainted empiricism and its adherents. These features are exhibited in exaggerated form by contemporary logicians like Wittgenstein who do not believe that the world exists apart from their sensations and ideas about it. As Wittgenstein says: "The world is my world," that is, reality is as I alone sense and interpret it.

Subjectivity in logical method is not confined to the philosophical faculties of Cambridge University. It crops up in the political thinking of people who never read a line of Hume, Russell, or Wittgenstein. Subjectivity in political matters springs from substituting purely personal feelings and reactions for an objective critical examination and rational appraisal of the decisive forces and factors at work in a given situation.

The correct criteria for judging the worth of a political figure should not be subjective and superficial reactions to his individual characteristics but the objective estimate of the class interests and purposes he and his party promote. A simple instance of misguided emotionalism was the support accorded by some workers to Churchill because of their admiration for his widely advertised grit. They overlooked the fundamental fact that this Tory bulldog was always the servant of monarchism and imperialism and a foe of the working people, at home and abroad.

In the late nineteen-fifties a number of ex-Communist and Socialist intellectuals, justly outraged by the exposures of Stalin's crimes, permitted these offenses of the ruling bureaucracy against socialism and the working class to becloud their judgment about the class nature of the Soviet Union. They saw nothing but the political abominations of the totalitarian regime and blinded themselves to the significance of the nationalized property and planned economy, which determine the fundamental content of Soviet society as a workers' state. They concluded that these conquests, which are at the base of the Soviet achievements, were not worth preserving and defending against imperialist aggression. Subjective reasoning of this type, however sincerely motivated, can thus lead to extremely reactionary political positions.

Many varieties of skepticism are rife among the bureaucrats and intellectuals in the Labour Party. Skepticism is not in and of itself evil, so long as it is not made the basis of a general philosophy. Doubts about God's existence can be the first step toward a materialist conception of the world; doubts about the longevity of capitalism can be the first step toward adherence to socialism.

The skepticism of the Labour reformists, however, is not used to dissolve and detach themselves from what is false, reactionary, and outmoded but to cast doubt on what is true, revolutionary, and progressive. They are not skeptical about the reality of the external world and man's capacity to know the truth about it, as are the current echoers of Hume. Where they manifest deep skepticism is about the *social* realities of our time. They doubt the future of the struggle for socialism and the capacities of the working class to direct and deal with economic and political affairs. They doubt the scientific solidity of Marxism and the validity of its philosophical foundations. Occasionally, they even doubt the validity of their own doubts.

This skepticism is the other side of their unspent confidence and lingering illusions in the capacities of the dying capitalist order to survive for an indefinite period.

The social roots of inconsistency

Everyone can sometimes fall victim to one or more of the vices of thought we have scrutinized. But this list of traits is not merely an abstract catalogue of universally shared psychological qualities or intellectual failings. They have a specific social basis and stamp. Taken as a whole, this assemblage of the errors of empirical thought are the hallmarks of a particular segment of bourgeois society: the middle classes.

When they attain political and ideological class consciousness, the polar groupings of capitalism, the monopolist rulers on top and the industrial workers down below, tend to acquire a homogeneity of views, of modes of thought, and types of conduct on the most vital issues. The peculiarity of the middle classes lies in the fact that the exceptional heterogeneity of their ideas and outlooks on social matters corresponds to the diversity in their conditions of life and the sharp contrasts and bewildering changes in their social situations. They are consistent, so to speak, only in their congenital inconsistency.

Trotsky once observed on this point: "Inconsistency is not accidental, and in politics it does not appear solely as an individual symptom. Inconsistency usually serves a social function. There are social groupings which cannot be consistent." (*In Defense of Marxism,* p. 112)

The in-between elements in the capitalist structure are bedeviled by inconsistency because they are constantly being tugged this way and that by the more integrated and powerful social forces of organized capital and organized labor pressing upon them. And they extend their vacillation and bewilderment into the ranks of the working class in many ways.

Two of the chief channels of confusion are the labor bureaucrats and the vacillating university intellectuals. Both are removed from the actual needs and everyday lives of the working people. Both fear to lose their privileges and break their associations with the established order; the second is reluctant to give up its vested interest in obsolete habits of thought. Both hold back the labor movement from acquiring a clear and consistent conception of its tasks and goals.

The socialist movement cannot get along without a world outlook and a method of thinking which has an internally logical theoretical structure from its premises to its conclusions, which is in agreement with both physical and social reality, and which accords with the interests and aims of the working class. Fortunately, it has such a philosophy in the dialectical materialism of the Marxist school.

Tradition and innovation

England is littered with encumbrances of the past which may delight the antiquarian and the tourist but hinder present progress. Stagecoach roads are unsuitable for speedy motor traffic. Many British factories are equipped with obsolete and inefficient machines. The political structure of England from the monarchy to the customs of the House of Commons is a mosaic of anachronisms.

There are likewise many archaic ideas in British heads. The British labor movement, which has grown up in this venerable capitalist environment, drags along with it a heavy load of prejudices from the bourgeois past. One of these anachronisms is its captivity to empirical ways of thought in coping with its problems.

The ideas of empiricism were once as novel and radical as are the ideas of Marxism today. They proved invaluable to the British bourgeoisie in its pioneering period. Since the capitalist regime this ruling class was constructing had immense historical aims to fulfill, the empirical mode of thought and its achievements benefited all humanity.

Empiricism continues to serve the bourgeoisie in its senility. But in the meantime both this class and its philosophy have become transformed. Capitalism has lost all reason for further existence, while the empirical methods of reasoning it sponsored have fallen far behind scientific and philosophical progress.

This philosophy cannot perform the same service for the working class in the replacement of capitalism as it did for the rising bourgeoisie in its creation. An obsolete type of thought can still be used to defend the old order; it is worthless for building a new one.

The disintegration of bourgeois society and the debacle of imperialism confront the British people with the need of overhauling their social structure from top to bottom. This revolutionary task involves, as it did in the seventeenth century, a thoroughgoing criticism of the traditional methods of thought and the introduction of new and better ones. Where are these new ideas to come from?

Fortunately, at this turning point in its career, the British working class does not have to improvise a philosophy from scratch. The basic theoretical equipment it needs has already been developed by revolutionary thinkers in other countries and tested by colossal historical events in our own time. It exists in the teachings of scientific socialism.

According to Lord Attlee, empiricism, with all its defects, ought to be retained because it is "in accord with the natural genius of the British people." However, this "natural genius" he speaks of is not an inherent and everlasting trait but the historical product of the favorable conditions of the bourgeois era.

What Attlee means is that empiricism is indigenous philosophy, whereas Marxism is a foreign import alien to the British temperament and traditions. This appeal to insular prejudice ignores some salient facts of British tradition itself. The militant forces of the seventeenth-century revolutions borrowed their Protestant creeds from the continent; the mechanical scientists were students of Galileo, Descartes, Gassendi, Huyghens, and others. The British bourgeoisie of Locke's time even deposed a home-grown dynasty and brought over a king from Holland to insure their sovereignty.

Why, then, should British labor hesitate to take what it now needs for its own purposes from other lands? If a Tory government can use the ideas of continental scientists in constructing atomic reactor plants and fabricating guided missiles, surely the labor movement is warranted in appropriating socialist science from other sections of the world working class to strengthen itself in the effort to establish a workers' regime in England.

But let us suppose that British history supplied no relevant precedents for such an action. Why should that keep labor from going ahead? "If there is no precedent for this, it is time to make one."

British politics has many examples of radical new departures. The innovators of the seventeenth century were not hamstrung by fealty to a dead past. The revolutionary democrats of the Leveller party appealed from the king and parliament to the direct action of the common people, the mass of the nation, for the first time. The regicides cut off the crowned head of a tyrant for the first time and developed a doctrine of natural rights and popular sovereignty to justify the deed. They disregarded the authority of precedent as ruthlessly as they rejected the precedent of established authority. British labor has the same right as its forerunners to forge its own precedents to gain its ends.

It is widely believed that labor can get along without any general theory of social development or its own revolutionary role in it. This illusion is a hangover from empiricism itself which depreciates the practical value of general ideas, especially in politics. If the working class operates without a principled guiding line of its own, it is bound to be misdirected by the views and pressures of other classes.

The labor movement can blunder along, as it has, without a broad world outlook. But it cannot fight effectively for its own interests and aims without a correct philosophical doctrine, any more than it can survive without its unions, political organizations, press, and educational facilities.

The Marxist criticism of empiricism goes hand in hand with opposition to reformism and opportunism in labor politics which reflect the influence of hostile social forces. In our time the working class has come forward in one country after another to challenge capitalism and replace its representatives in all fields of social life, from the organization and control of industry to the administration of government.

The realm of theory cannot be an exception to this rule. The universal contest between bourgeois traditions and working-class innovations is also being fought out where their respective philosophical outlooks and logical methods are being thought out and applied.

Marxism has already been adopted as its guide by the labor vanguard in many countries. It has spread throughout the world because it has proved in action to be the sole method of thought which measures up to the demands of our century and can orient the working class correctly in its domestic struggles and the complexities of the world situation.

Dialectical materialism is the scientific expression of

the international working-class movement on its way to the conquest of political sovereignty and the remaking of society. It is the theoretical outlook of the revolutionary transition from the capitalist past to the communist future. On the plane of philosophy it corresponds to the passage from the steam engine to nuclear energy in motive power, from the internal combustion motor to the jet plane in transport, from private property to public ownership of the means of production, from capitalist exploitation and anarchy to planned production on a world scale, from bourgeois rule to working-class democracy.

Its further diffusion would provide an antidote to the theoretical anemia and national narrow-mindedness that hold back the advance of labor. It has to be recognized that the cherished empirical habits of thought belong among such antiquities as the monarchy, the established church, muskets, and tiewigs. They are as outdated as British domination of the world market, unregulated trade, the workhouse, and middle-class liberalism. They are as much out of line with the most progressive trends in scientific and social matters as the methods of Conservative and right-wing Labour foreign policy.

The conscious assimilation of the teachings of dialectical materialism would bring the thought of the vanguard of British socialism abreast of countries which have traveled farther along the revolutionary road. Its ideas, skillfully and scrupulously applied to the specific conditions of British life, would not only clarify the problems of its labor movement but contribute to the enrichment of scientific socialism itself. In this way the materialist method of Marxism could become, in the remainder of the twentieth century, as secure an acquisition of progressive British culture as the methods of empiricism were in the revolutionary heyday of the capitalist epoch.

9

Pragmatism and empiricism

Barrows Dunham has observed in *Thinkers and Treasurers* that middle-class philosophy is highly competitive and pluralistic. It is possible and permissible for a professor to be a pragmatist, a positivist, a realist, an idealist, an existentialist, or any shading or combination of these. However, this free enterprise in ideas has its limits. "Those limits are medieval philosophy on the one hand and Marxist philosophy on the other. The life of Western philosophy and the lives of its philosophers are spent in trying not to go back to the thirteenth century and not to go forward to the twenty-first."

This is certainly true of American philosophy. It has spontaneously spurned scholasticism, since it was born after the rise of bourgeois society, the victories of the democratic revolutions, and under the auspices of Protestantism. Thanks to the expansion and stability of capitalism in this country, it has yet to arrive at an acceptance and assimilation of dialectical materialism.

The central and characteristic philosophy of the American people has been, and remains to this day, one or another form of pragmatism. The pragmatic outlook and mode of thought had deep roots in the special conditions of the development of bourgeois civilization and culture in North America. It was created as a distinctive theory at the turn of the twentieth century as the philosophical expression and instrument of that middle-class liberalism which was politically embodied in the Progressive protests against plutocratic domination.

Its principal ideas were derived from the events, forces, and views of the bourgeois-democratic movements of the Western world and the First American Revolution. Its theory of knowledge stemmed from John Locke. Its conception of society as based on a social contract, which could be remodeled by the common consent of all citizens, originated in the ideas of Roger Williams, Rousseau, Paine, Jefferson, and similar advocates of the doctrine of "natural rights." Its political program harked back to the ideals voiced in the Declaration of Independence.

In its ideological genealogy, pragmatism is essentially a belated and updated branch of the empirical tradition which has been the main stream of philosophy among the English-speaking peoples for over three centuries. Empiricism, pragmatism, and instrumentalism, or its variant, "operationalism," represent three consecutive phases in the evolution of the same trend of thought. Empiricism was the matrix, the rudimentary and general form from which pragmatism sprang, while Dewey's instrumentalism is the highest expression of pragmatism.

Why and how did the pragmatists remodel British empiricism?

The body of empirical theory as it was handed down to the founders of pragmatism at the end of the nineteenth century suffered from obvious shortcomings in their eyes. First, its account of the process of acquiring knowledge kept the body and its senses far too passive. These were pictured as inactive recipients or reflectors of whatever was impressed upon them from without. "In naked perception the mind is, for the most part, merely passive," wrote Locke. The reactions of the human organism to external stimuli, the modifications of these stimuli in the nervous system, and the activity of the mental processes were largely overlooked or slighted.

Classical empiricism was far less concerned with the *forms* of knowledge than with the origins and validity of its *content*. The German idealists correctly criticized the empiricists, both for ignoring the active powers of the sensibility and the thought processes and for disregarding the specific forms of knowledge in its development. They undertook to examine these sides of knowledge in opposition to the teachings of empiricism.

The pragmatists James and Dewey, who came long after them, tried to remedy these defects without going beyond the bounds of empiricism. Dewey, for example, sought to provide a more dynamic basis for the empirical theory of cognition with the aid of Darwinism, James' psychology, and some insights borrowed from Hegel.

Second, the original empiricism was unhistorical and nonevolutionary. This was a shortcoming it shared with other branches of science in that epoch. Locke's *An Essay Concerning Human Understanding* analyzes the foundations, structure, and verification of knowledge without attempting to review the historical process by which human understanding comes into existence, the stages through which it had to pass, or the specific phase it had entered. He appeals not to evidence taken from a study of biological and social processes, but "to men's own unprejudiced experiences and observations."

The pragmatists were evolutionists. They undertook to show how the organs of knowledge and knowledge itself originated in animal life and had been accumulated and improved as humanity developed. They resorted to new findings in the sciences of biology and psychology for those purposes.

An even deeper defect of classical empiricism was its failure to explain the influence of the *social* environment and its changes upon the origins and evolution of man's knowledge. Bacon, Locke, and Hume assumed that men's minds had functioned in precisely the same ways from time immemorial and that the processes of thought were governed by the same kind of fixed and universal laws as the movements of the heavenly bodies. For them human nature was essentially invariant.

The pragmatists knew better and looked upon human nature as plastic and variable. However, they did not probe to the bottom for the social and historical causes of the changes in human capacities, characteristics, and ideas. James, for example, ascribed the diversities in men's philosophies to different types of temperament. Dewey was more profound and historical-minded. He turned to anthropology and the primitive modes of occupation to explain the savage mind. He referred to the class stratifications of Greek slave society to account for the special traits of Aristotle's logic and cosmology. But he never grasped the essence of the materialist method of historical explanation or applied it with any consistency.

Finally, classical empiricism was extremely individualistic. Its theory of knowledge took its point of departure from the experience of the solitary individual divorced from his fellow men. Dewey especially made energetic efforts to overcome this intractable individualism by bringing into his structure of thought the social nature of the conditioning, thinking, and functioning of the separate personality.

In addition to renovating empiricism by removing some of its archaisms and inadequacies and revising its doctrines in the light of later scientific developments and data, pragmatism redirected the line of its interests. The motives and aims of the American pragmatists were quite different from those of the founders of British empiricism. Locke, Hobbes, and Hume were primarily concerned with the *origin* of our ideas. They sought answers to the questions, Where do our ideas come from and what guarantees their validity? Although they gave somewhat different solutions to these problems, they followed a common procedure of tracing ideas back to their roots in sensation, reflection, or a combination of both processes, and they tried to find the warrant for the correctness of ideas in previous experience.

Their descendants, James and Dewey, came upon the scene at a much later stage in the evolution of empiricism, when its fruits had not only ripened but had become somewhat decayed. These latter-day empiricists took for granted the ready-made premises of their school: the sensory origin of ideas, the nonexistence of innate principles, etc., and preoccupied themselves with an entirely different set of questions.

They did not ask, Where do our ideas come from? That was for them a settled question. They inquired, Where do our ideas go to and what are they good for? Instead of asking, How did ideas originate and what are their roots? they asked, What functions do they perform and what effects do they have upon further experience? They were, so to speak, primarily interested in the distribution and destination of ideas rather than in the sources and conditions of their production.

This change of emphasis was clearly discernible in the address delivered by William James in 1898, when he recast Peirce's pragmatic formula for obtaining clear ideas in these words: "To attain perfect clearness in our thoughts of an object, then, we need only consider what *effects* of a conceivably *practical* kind the object may involve and what sensations we may *expect* from it, and what reactions we must *prepare*. Our conception of their effects, then, is for us the whole of our conception of the object, so far as that conception has positive significance at all." (My emphasis)

The emphasized words indicate clearly enough the pronounced shift of attention from causes to consequences, from material grounds to practical effects, from determined conditions to expectation, from correspondence of ideas with realities to preparation for action that are the hallmarks of the pragmatic theory of knowledge.

The pragmatists were faithful to the empiricist tradition in announcing that they were giving to the world not a new conception of being, but merely a new theory of knowledge and an improved definition of truth and error. In his popular exposition of pragmatism, William James called it "a new name for some old ways of thinking." He characterized pragmatism as an attitude of mind, a mode of thought, a point of view, rather than a theory of reality or a system of the world.

In addition to assuming a new name, the Yankee pragmatists added five significant amendments to the charter of traditional British empiricism.

First, they stressed the biological origins and nature of mental phenomena. The pragmatists asserted that intelligence and ideas were rooted in animal life and must be approached as the outgrowth and extension of biological processes.

Second, they emphasized the practical functions of ideas. According to the pragmatists, the chief service performed by the mind was to help men achieve their ends. Intelligence arose out of the practical difficulties encountered in everyday life, intervened as a discoverer of possibilities in a troubled situation and as an indicator of effective solutions to its problems. Thereby, mind played a constructive, or rather a reconstructive, role in the processes of experience.

Third, the founders of pragmatism took exception to the assumption of the British empiricists that sense data are intrinsically isolated. In the theory of perception presented by James and Dewey, both connections *and* distinctions were given together in immediate experience. This recognition of the cohesiveness of sense experience enabled the pragmatists to avoid some of the difficulties engendered by the fictitious unrelatedness of each single sense impression which had led to Hume's skepticism.

Fourth, the pragmatists looked upon ideas as *purposive* and *prospective.* The real content of concepts is not determined by what has gone into them through previous experience or through what is given them by objective reality. This merely conditions ideas. Their final and real content is determined by what comes out of them when they are acted upon and their consequences in practice are observed and known. Ideas do not look backward, outward, or inward; they look and lead forward. They are all permeated with human purpose. Concepts are habits of belief which become habits of action, not reflections of realities.

Finally, the pragmatists defined truth as a quality which is acquired by ideas solely in practice. The validity of an idea is not determined by its correspondence with independent and prior real conditions, which is then tested in practice. The truth of an idea is derived from and through practical experience. Ideas in themselves are nothing but "working hypotheses" which have to acquire their truth as well as demonstrate it by their effectiveness in solving the problems and realizing the aims of men.

These five propositions summarize the main points of the pragmatic theory of knowledge as well as the novelties it introduced into classical empiricism.

The pragmatists, like the empiricists before them, used their innovations as weapons for polemics on two fronts. On one side they took up the cudgels against the idealists who refused to admit the natural origins and practical functions of the thought processes and who defended unchanging principles and the purely speculative, logical, and contemplative essence of reason. By hammering away at these bulwarks of idealist error, the pragmatists helped bring philosophy closer to reality and the results of scientific discovery.

However, the pragmatists directed more of their criticism against the materialist conception of the unity of being and thought. They agreed with the materialist premise that mind was an outgrowth of nature and society but violently rejected the materialist conclusions that its contents must conform to the reality of nature and society and be ultimately derived from them.

For pragmatism, ideas were not determined by an objective independent world nor did they reflect its features; ideas were made and remade in the course of experience by the needs and will of man. This one-sided, subjectivist notion of the nature of ideas and of truth was hailed by its proponents and admirers as an epoch-making advance in philosophy. Actually, it was a step backward, not only from the advanced ground attained by the progress of materialism, but even from the position of Locke.

William James

Let us see how this worked out in the thought of William James, the ardent popularizer of pragmatism. The Harvard professor proclaimed himself to be "a radical empiricist." He wrote in *Essays in Radical Empiricism:* "To be radical, an empiricist must neither admit into his constructions any element that is not directly experienced, nor exclude from them any element that is directly experienced." This is the same rule that Hume adopted as his guide.

What then, according to James, do we directly experience? Nothing but "pure experience" which is "the immediate flux of life which furnishes the material to our later reflection." This "pure experience" is the primal stuff out of which everything else is subsequently composed. It exists before either matter or mind. These are only extracted or constructed later as separate functions of the featureless flowing stream.

James thus sought to efface the priority of the external world over the mind and the essential difference between the objective and subjective, the known and the knower. For him there is not an external world existing before mankind or our relations with it, which are then experienced and thought about. The world is created by mankind out of the formless plastic mass of "pure experience" which precedes anything and everything else. Mankind takes the place of God in Genesis, creating the world and its distinctive divisions out of the primal flux of events.

It is true that the objective and subjective are inseparable in mankind and that the world first appears to us as "a buzzing, blooming confusion." But mankind and its experiences are not identical or coexistent with material existence; they are a product and part of its evolution.

James reverses the real relations between experience

and reality. He makes nature depend upon experience, not experience upon nature. The root of his error is in identifying the subjective aspects of human experience with the objective existence of the world—and then drowning the latter in the former.

His theory of knowledge and interpretation of the truth depend upon the doctrine of "pure experience." If experience comes before nature, then ideas do not copy external reality. Ideas are primarily plans of action. They enable us to operate advantageously in relation to other things; they are means of orientation in the flux of pure experience, guiding us along in it and helping us make the most of its currents. Out of them we build our picture of the world.

How do we separate true ideas from the false? Not by testing their conformity with given realities but by conceiving what their effects would be and noting the consequences when we act upon them. If an idea does help us get along in this stream of experience, fulfills our needs, satisfies our desires and demands, then it is true, or rather it becomes true to that extent. "An idea is 'true' so long as to believe it is profitable to our lives." And "the true is only the expedient in the way of our thinking . . . in the long run and on the whole, of course."

This "expediency" interpretation of truth and falsehood is bound up with a special version of the nature of human action. All activity for James is fundamentally experimental in character, a gamble. We try out this idea or that, this procedure or that, and then see what happens. If it does the assigned job, well and good; if it fails, try something else. "If at first you don't succeed, try, try again."

The whole flux of experience is thereby subjected to determination by human action alone, apart from objective circumstances. This is a highly subjective conception of the interplay of ideas and experience. Collective human action can, to be sure, decide many things in life, up to the further development of society. But it can do so only when it proceeds in consonance with the material possibilities of the historically given objective conditions, and not in any arbitrary manner that runs counter to them.

But human activity by itself doesn't determine either the nature of things or the nature of ideas. These are by and large determined for us, not by us. James had a different opinion.

He used this pragmatic conception of ideas as nothing but "working hypotheses," and truth as shaped by the consequences of human action and aims, as a springboard for the justification of religion. "We cannot reject any hypothesis if consequences useful to life flow from it . . . if the hypothesis of God works satisfactorily in the widest sense of the word, it is true . . ." And he finds that religious experience affords proof "that higher powers exist and are at work to save the world on ideal lines similar to our own."

James thus went back to Bishop Berkeley who likewise used the doctrine of "pure experience" to demolish skepticism, materialism, and atheism and hand the world over to God's jurisdiction. There are not a few such "impure" elements in the alleged "pure experience" of the pragmatists; the new dish they served contained some old and rather odorous ingredients.

By starting with the premises of Hume and ending close to the conclusions of Berkeley, James showed how retrogressive empiricism had become in its refurbished pragmatic version. Compared with Locke, and still more with Bacon, he took several steps backward since the momentum of his philosophy and its results were different from theirs. Although they too retained a personal belief in God's existence, the effect of their philosophical activity was to loosen reason and science from the grip of religion and make room for the advance of the most progressive thought of their age.

More than two hundred years after this release, James explicitly tried to reconnect philosophy with religion, thus substituting irrationalism for the exercise of reason and involuntarily promoting obscurantism. Philosophy was once again supposed to serve as a handmaiden of religious faith. "Let empiricism once become associated with religion, as hitherto, through some strange misunderstanding, it has been associated with irreligion and I believe that a new era of religion as well as of philosophy will be ready to begin," James asserted in *The Varieties of Religious Experience.* Such a relapse would have undone the work accomplished by the most enlightened advocates of classical empiricism from Locke to Hume.

John Dewey

John Dewey was less of an individualist and less concerned with salvaging crumbling religious certainties than his co-thinker, William James. As the major philosopher of Progressivism, he was the most collectivist representative of the pragmatic school and even espoused in later life a mild brand of evolutionary socialism.

Dewey explicitly acknowledged that empiricism was the parent of pragmatism and was proud of their kinship. "We must not forget here," he wrote in *Philosophy and Civilization,* "that James was an empiricist before he was a pragmatist, and repeatedly stated that pragmatism is merely empiricism pushed to its legitimate conclusion." Throughout his work he constantly appealed to the premises and propositions of the empirical tradition while claiming to be eliminating its errors and defects.

Dewey broke most sharply with classical empiricism in regard to the nature of sensation and the part it played in the process of knowledge. Locke, following Bacon and Hobbes, maintained that all human knowledge came from and was based upon the action of external material objects upon the sense organs which produced simple ideas. These sense data form "the materials of all our knowledge."

Dewey turned this cardinal principle of the empirical theory of knowledge inside out. Whereas for Locke sensation was the source and foundation of cognition, for Dewey sensation was completely noncognitive. "Sentiency in itself is anoetic," he stated in *Experience and Nature* (p. 259). The phenomena of sense simply have a quality of immediacy which, as such, is senseless and conveys no meaning. "Things in their immediacy are unknown and unknowable, not because they are remote or behind some impenetrable veil of sensation or ideas, but because knowledge has no concern with them," he argued (*Ibid.*, p. 86). Sensations are simply "had," suffered, and enjoyed; they are not in anyway known.

The notion that "sensations are cases of knowledge" is "a superstition, growing up in a false physics and physiology and perpetuated by psychology . . ." Dewey wrote in *Essays in Experimental Logic* (p. 262). Perceptions have no inherent validity or cognitive value; they are no more than "natural events, having in themselves . . . no more knowledge status or worth than, say, a shower or a fever . . ." (*Ibid.*, p. 253)

This contention that sensations are merely natural events having no essential connection with cognition of the external world is disproved by the evolutionary origins and development of our sense organs and their functions. The sensibility of the higher nervous system, which has grown in the higher animals out of the irritability of lower organisms, as Dewey himself noted, is the outcome of the action of external causes on the living creature. Vision has emerged from the phototropism by which a plant or simple organism turns to the light and follows its course. Eyes would never have developed without the pre-existence of light rays, which act upon the body whose organ of vision is the means of reacting to them.

In the act of vision, luminous energy from a specific material source becomes converted into nervous energy which, through complex psycho-physical processes in the cerebral cortex, generates the image of qualities of external objects. Thus objective physical properties become transformed into subjective impressions, or what Locke called a "simple idea."

We are aware of the forms of matter in motion only through the sensations which they produce on our sense organs. Bats, gliding on silent wings, have an ultrasonic "sonar" system to avoid obstacles and intercept insects. This sound apparatus enables the bat to receive and interpret vital information concerning its environment. If sight and hearing had no connection with their sources in the external world and conveyed no information about them, eyes and ears would have been useless in the struggle for existence and would never have been developed by birds or men.

Living beings have developed only those sense organs and their capacities which were necessary to preserve the species and enhance its adaptability. If sensations did not reflect the properties of reality, how could sensation enable animals and men to orient themselves and adapt themselves effectively to their surroundings and its continual changes? How would animals survive if, for example, they could not recognize food through their senses and distinguish what was edible from what was unassimilable?

Sensation is not merely a stimulus to action, as Dewey believed, but the crudest form of knowledge—its raw material. It is the most vital and central link in the unity of the organism with the external conditions of its existence.

The impulses emanating from some section of the external world impinging upon the organism excites a motor response, an unconditioned reflex, which is the basis and beginning of all subsequent and higher forms of knowledge, from conditioned reflexes through perceptions to concepts and laws.

Dewey's denial that sensation has any intrinsically cognitive elements even of the lowest kind is an extreme expression of the subjectivist trend in the empirical tradition fostered by Hume. By severing the sensory ties between the organism and its environment, Dewey removed the genetic unity between what objectively exists and what is experienced. This opened the way for the affirmation of the fundamental thesis of the pragmatic and instrumentalist theory of knowledge that ideas do not disclose the content of reality but are invested with truth by human action alone.

The instrumentalist epistemology is detached from objective reality at both ends of the acquisition of knowledge. In its origins, sensation is regarded as without cognitive links with the external world; in its ultimate results, concepts allegedly enable us to reshape things without necessarily corresponding in any respect with the content of reality.

Thus Dewey's discarding of the empirical principle that sensation was the ground of knowledge served to accentuate and consummate the departure from objectivity prefigured in the pristine ambiguity of empiricism about the relations between our sensations and their material causes.

Despite their departures from classical empiricism in certain respects, the pragmatists did not break away from its prime postulate that what is presented here and now to the individual affords the best insight into the nature of reality. Pragmatism remained attached to the phenomenology of experience. The mandates of its method inhibited persistent search for the inner causal connections in the full scope of their evolution which generate the outward appearances of things.

James and Dewey not only tried to bring traditional empiricism abreast of the scientific achievements of the nineteenth century. They remodeled its ideas to suit the requirements and outlook of the liberal middle-class intellectuals of their day. Indeed, the pragmatic philosophy had the same relation to empiricism as the political program of Progressivism had to capitalism and bourgeois democracy. It aspired to modernize the structure rather than change the foundations.

The modifications introduced by pragmatism did not succeed in eradicating the inherent and insuperable defects of empiricism but rather reaffirmed them in its own way. The dualism between materialism and idealism discernible in Locke flowered into eclecticism with Dewey. As an illustration, take his treatment of the relations between the social system and the philosopher himself.

Dewey did not hesitate to apply the principle of historical materialism that a thinker's views are fundamentally shaped by his social situation and class outlook to explain the special features and errors of Aristotle's metaphysics and politics. Yet he claimed that his own philosophy was totally exempt from class conditioning and that he spoke for the general interests of all men. The coexistence of two such incompatible types of interpretation did not disconcert him; he used either one as he pleased.

Dewey was the most radical consummator of the pragmatic tendency. He did for pragmatism what pragmatism helped to do for the empirical tradition. His instrumentalism pressed its ideas to the farthest limits and thereby disclosed their basic insufficiency. Empiricism cannot go beyond Deweyism without annulling its basic premises and either passing over into materialism to its left or towards logical positivism or linguistic analysis to its right.

10

Materialism and empiricism today

The materialist conception of the world is squarely opposed not to empiricism, but to idealism. Empiricism is a composite of ideas belonging to dissimilar and even incompatible viewpoints; it is situated between these polar types of philosophy.

The heterogeneous and unstable character of empiricism makes it difficult to pin down the positions of its representatives with precision. Some place the chief emphasis on the more materialist aspects of this school; others give predominance to its idealist possibilities. To heap up confusion, either tendency can slide over to the opposite side on certain issues.

Consequently the relations between empiricism and materialism over the past four centuries have been extremely variable and complicated. The revival of materialist doctrines coincided with the birth of empiricism in the seventeenth century. They were cognate instruments of the revolutionary bourgeois culture. Although materialism was a more uncompromising adversary of the old forms of thought, it was itself incomplete and inharmonious. At the same time its spokesmen collaborated with the empiricists in vindicating the ideas and methods of the new scientific outlook against medieval authorities and feudal obscurantism as well as against mysticism and idealism.

The materialism of Bacon and Hobbes was refracted through Locke's writings and transmitted to such outstanding materialist minds of the eighteenth century as Toland, Hartley, and Priestley in England; Condillac, Helvetius, Holbach, and Diderot in France; and Thomas Cooper in North America. Locke can be legitimately regarded both as a continuator of British materialism and as the fountainhead of the departures from this standpoint by his empirical followers. His belief in the causal role of material things in the genesis of sensations and ideas warranted stricter materialist conclusions. On the other hand, his wobbling on the crucial question of the relation of ideas to the objective world dislodged the empirical theory of knowledge from a firm anchorage in reality and left it susceptible to agnostic and idealist uses.

All these variants emerged in the next stage of the evolution of the empirical school. The eighteenth century brought forth a spectrum of tendencies ranging from Berkeley's subjective idealism at one end to the sensationalism of the French materialists of the Enlightenment at the other. It often happens that ideas which are placidly absorbed in more advanced countries have explosive effects when transplanted into more retarded environments. Locke's foreign influence in the eighteenth century had this subversive character. The materialist implications of Locke's views in epistemology and political theory were eagerly seized upon and developed by radical thinkers in

France, America, and other countries that were heading toward or passing through their own bourgeois revolutions.

The ascendancy and conservatizing of the bourgeois regimes in the nineteenth century tended to brush aside the more materialist elements and exponents of empiricism and bring the skeptical conclusions of Hume to the fore. His reasonings against the reality of causation, the existence of substance, and the objectivity of scientific knowledge frayed the materialist ties of classical empiricism, made possible a reinstatement of religious belief through irrational faith, and steered many empiricists onto the paths of agnosticism and, in extreme cases, subjective idealism.

However much the rapid advances of natural science augmented knowledge and reinforced the truths of materialism, almost all the empirically tutored thinkers of that era refused to be identified with its doctrines. Typical was "Darwin's bulldog," the biologist T.H. Huxley, who had a materialist conception of nature and man's position in it and held that all our knowledge is based on information derived from the senses. Yet he was deterred by the influence of Hume's and Kant's arguments, and by the opprobrium attached to materialism by British respectability, from asserting that sense perceptions disclose the essence of material reality. He took refuge in an agnosticism which Engels characterized as "shame-faced materialism."

Since Huxley's time, the more popular varieties of empiricism have accentuated their nonmaterialist features. The distance between the two philosophies has been widened by the persistent challenge offered by the systematic materialist teachings of Marxism to all forms of equivocation and confusion on the principal problems of philosophy prevalent among the empiricists. They in turn have defined their positions in more conscious repulsion against dialectical materialism. This antagonism has been most sharply manifested in the social and political arena, where the confrontations between liberalism and socialism, reformism and revolutionary action, have been tied up with adherence to the rival methods of empiricism and positivism or Marxism.

Thus, starting out as intimate associates in the struggle against medievalism, the two schools of thought now stand arrayed against each other in fields extending from method in natural science to sociology and politics.

Positivism in epistemology

Materialism and classical empiricism were joined together by their acceptance of the principles that all knowledge comes from the senses and depends upon the material conditions of life. Hegel discerned these ties of affinity from his idealist vantage point. He declared in his *Logic* that a "systematically carried through" empiricism leads to materialism. He correctly saw that for both schools the objective facts disclosed by sense perception take precedence over thought, which is a derivative phenomenon.

Materialism differed from empiricism not in denying those truths in its theory of knowledge, which they shared, but by developing their necessary consequences without reservation or restriction. Marxism did not criticize the empiricist school for maintaining the principles which both opposed to all forms of idealism, but for the failure of the empiricists to stick to them and rigorously apply them. The empiricists also took a too mechanical, one-sided, and static view of the facts and, through their incomplete and inconsistent account of reality, arrived at arbitrary and misleading conclusions.

Hegel had in mind the more materialist views of Locke

rather than the skeptical and subjectivist interpretations of his latter-day disciples. He would have been exceedingly scornful of their refusal to reconcile reason with reality and knowledge with objectivity, which he regarded as the prime task of philosophizing. It was precisely this congenital incapacity to bring the objective and subjective sides of human experience into concordance with each other that has so vitiated contemporary empiricism and widened its breach with modern materialism.

Although their differences have become deeper and more definitive, the main line of division between the two philosophies remains the same as it was in the beginning; it concerns the theory of knowledge, the nature of truth and error. While both agree on the proposition that all knowledge is based on sensation, they diverge over the answer to the question, What is it that the senses know?

Materialism teaches that the senses provide authentic information about the external world. There is a rough but reliable correspondence between the relations, operations, and features of reality and the content of our ideas about them. This correspondence, or lack of it, is what makes concepts, theories, laws, hypotheses true or renders them false.

By and large, contemporary empiricists are much vaguer and more ambiguous on what the senses tell us and what the actual connections are between our ideas and the world around us. They submit a wide variety of responses to these problems, depending upon their particular turn of thought: agnostic (we do not know what is really given); skeptical (we cannot know what reality is); idealistic and subjectivist in sensationalist terms (all we know are our sensations which reveal nothing beyond ourselves). Whatever their differences with one another, all shades of empirical opinion unite in rejecting a clear-cut stand on the key issues of epistemology. They incline to postpone or evade any affirmative or negative answer on whether sense experience provides objective truths about the external world.

This problem persists and cannot be once for all settled because the circumference of knowledge keeps extending. Whenever and wherever scientific research makes a big breakthrough on the frontiers of knowledge and plumbs deeper into the labyrinths of reality, the old controversy recurs on a higher level. Just as Locke was unsure whether man could ever know the underlying material causes of qualities, so some nineteenth-century scientists and philosophers questioned the real existence of molecules and atoms.

Now that the objective reality of these parts of matter has been convincingly confirmed, similar doubts are raised about subatomic phenomena. Are the "strongly interacting particles" real or fictitious, material or mental? Materialist-minded physicists hold that, on the basis of the already available evidence, the so-called "elementary particles" objectively exist. They can be counted, their tracks can be followed, and they meet other experimental tests.

Of course, their number as well as their relations, properties, and activities are far from being accurately ascertained or fully described. Some hypothetical tentative conclusions about them will have to be revised or discarded as investigation continues. But the real existence of these tiny units of matter has been attested to in numerous ways by scientific procedures.

On the other hand, many positivists contend that elementary particles are not facts but idealized concepts, abstractions, models, analogies, theoretical constructs. They do not have a physical but a purely mental status.

This controversy can be resolved only by the weight of

the facts on one side or the other. The ether of the nineteenth century was found to be an arbitrary hypothesis, a purely conceptual invention. The atom, on the other hand, which Mach classified as no more than a useful fiction, has turned out to be undeniably material. It took deeper experimental probing into the recesses of reality to decide that the one was imaginary and the other objectively existent. The right of the facts to determine the status of all ideas in men's minds accords with the mandates of the materialist theory of knowledge.

Curiously, the positivists are more likely to doubt the materiality of microphenomena than the reality of astrophysical events, even though our data on these might have come through radioscopes from eight thousand million light years away. Apparently agnosticism builds a nest among the obscurities of the infinitesimal more readily than in the far reaches of the universe. But this nest is constantly being disturbed by more verified information.

The epistemological inhibitions of empiricism, especially in its positivistic guises, exert a paralyzing effect upon its adherents. They become tied to the surface of things, inclined toward passive acceptance of the status quo in science and society, and restrained from extending knowledge beyond its present boundaries to more profound levels of reality. This hesitancy to get behind immediate appearances and go beyond the existing state of affairs is still more pronounced in respect to the problems of society than those of natural science. There is much more at stake.

Positivism in sociology

Does history have any regularities that can be scientifically known and used to foresee and shape the future? Marxism says yes, positivism says no, to this cardinal question of sociology.

Both the positivists and their ideological cousins, the pragmatists, are extremely dubious about the existence of sociological laws and the possibilities of ascertaining the direction of social developments. They disavow historical determinism, especially in connection with the prospects of capitalism, and are intent upon disqualifying the claims of Marxism to be scientific.

Their case is most vigorously argued nowadays by Professor Karl Popper of the University of London, author of *The Open Society and its Enemies, The Logic of Scientific Discovery,* and *The Poverty of Historicism.* This influential theorist of positivist method in the social sciences is a proponent of "piecemeal social engineering." He is also a pioneer of cold-war liberalism whose reputation in the West has been enhanced by the political consequences of his views. As early as 1945 he expounded the thesis that the central issue of our time was the world conflict between capitalist democracy and communist totalitarianism, the first safeguarding the values of reason, freedom, democracy, individualism, and liberalism in "an open society," the other promoting collectivism, servitude, and authoritarianism in "a closed society." The contending camps had their respective philosophies in a flexible empiricism versus a dogmatic dialectical materialism.

Professor Popper is not conservative but progressive in his social outlook. He expresses agreement with Marx that philosophers should not simply interpret the world but help change it. He contends, however, that Marxist historical method is not suited for that purpose; its pretentions to scientific knowledge of the laws of social development are spurious.

Although Professor Popper believes in a kind of physical necessity, he does not extend any determinism to social phenomena. In an address on "Prediction and Prophecy in the Social Sciences," delivered at the Tenth International Congress of Philosophy at Amsterdam, 1948, and printed in *Theories of History,* edited by Patrick Gardiner, he asserts that "there exists no law of evolution" either for plants and animals or for man. Consequently there is no factual basis for forecasting economic, political, or historical developments. He labels the irrepressible fondness for prediction shared by diverse schools of sociology as "historicism" and focuses his attack upon Marxism as the worst offender in the practice of "futurism."

Scientific socialism maintains that the purpose of both natural and social science is to know in order to foresee correctly and act most effectively. That is its practical value, the reason why so many people devote so much time to scientific work and governments today subsidize it so heavily.

Professor Popper dismisses this aim in sociology as wishful thinking. It is the modern secular version of an age-old dream of prophecy—"the idea that we can know what the future has in store for us, and that we can profit from such knowledge by adjusting our policy to it." The kind of predictability pursued by historical materialists, who believe that human affairs are causally determined and lawful, is a chimera because history exhibits no dependable regularities, he says. It is largely made up of singular cases. "Non-repetitive events are the most striking aspects of historical development," he writes.

Obviously, no general laws can be derived from an endless series of purely unique events. If every occurrence in social life and the procession of history was as unprecedented as he proclaims, scientific analysis would indeed be impossible. So would any reasonable orientation and effective action.

Positivism claims to be superior to dialectical materialism because it is not dogmatic but faithful to the facts. The rival theories may therefore be tested by reference to the basic facts about the regularities and irregularities of social existence and historical development.

The society around the professor does undergo minor modifications from day to day but, barring overnight revolutions, he can count on meeting substantially the same institutions and customs in the morning as when he fell asleep on the previous evening. But he has not awakened to the philosophical import of this simple fact.

It is grossly unfactual to assert that history has no reliable regularities or that nonrepetitive events are its decisive characteristics. Social relations themselves refute such a contention; they are definite types of perennially repeated mutual interactions among men arising from continuous activities of a definite kind. The regularities of society are primarily expressed in the productive activities and economic relations of its members. Since our species emerged from the primate stage, men have acquired and produced the means of satisfying their needs in routine ways through repetitive labor processes. The tools they made for that purpose were fashioned according to traditional techniques and previous models.

Our prime source of knowledge about preliterate times comes from archaeology, that science of society which deals with the earliest human activities incorporated in artifacts. Although each of these products and instruments of labor has individual characteristics, almost all belong to specific types. "If the implement be unique, it is not a datum for archaeology at all; it remains just a curio, until a similar implement, that is, one of the same type, be observed in a significant archaeological context . . . Archaeologists must ignore the small individual peculiarities of any given knife and treat it as an instance of one or another of the standard types, as a member of that class of knives," observes V. Gordon Childe in *A Short Introduction to Archaeology* (pp. 13–14).

Jacquetta Hawkes tells us that "in the Lower Paleolithic period the hand-axe, although it was gradually improved, remained in use as the dominant tool form for over a quarter of a million years." (*Prehistory*, p. 172)

The social relations of the most primitive peoples were as simple and standardized as their instruments of production. The small bands or tribes of Stone Age food-gatherers, hunters or fishermen, had collectivist institutions and customs. The scope of variations in their social organization were held within the narrow limits prescribed by their mode of production. They might live in caves or camps but had, as a rule, no permanent settlements.

The innovation of food production which gave rise to barbarism introduced the first epoch-making changes and extensive diversifications into primitive social structures. But the barbaric communities and kingdoms were based upon agriculture. What could be more repetitive than this kind of economy rooted in the natural processes of plant growth and reproduction, regulated by the round of the seasons, and carried on by traditional techniques and rituals?

Mankind took more than a million years to go from savagery through barbarism to civilization. This crawling pace indicates how greatly recurrences outweighed novelties in daily life. Even after the most advanced sections of humanity became civilized, the fixity of social relations and the slow and intermittent rate of change in the agricultural societies, culminating in feudalism, betokened the predominance of repetition in the lives and labors of their human constituents.

Change becomes the rule rather than the exception in society and history only with the advent of capitalism—precisely because of the peculiar nature of its mode of production. Unlike previous master classes, the bourgeoisie is impelled by the dictates of its economic interests to keep modernizing and revolutionizing the conditions of production. This is imposed by competition, the necessities of capital accumulation, the drive for the maximization of profits. Incidentally, that is why the peasant is "historyless," the proletariat is so historical-minded, and theorists like Professor Popper are so preoccupied with the problem of changeability.

However, bourgeois changeability has inherent limits. As much as the capitalist class may reform the economy and other parts of society, it cannot replace the mode of production and appropriation upon which its property, profits, and power rest. It must safeguard these at all costs. This conservative basis of its socioeconomic position clashes with the cumulative changes in the rest of the system. The intensification of these contradictions in its system has led to grave social and political crises that have already resulted in the overturn of capitalist relations in countries on three continents.

What about the nonrecurrent features of events? These may be interesting and dramatic, but they cannot be the decisive causal factors, the main determinants and driving forces of history, however much they affect the particular occurrence. Random events are usually the unessential, accessory, incidental, superficial, and trivial aspects of the historical process.

However, this is not always the case. Qualitatively new events or deviations from the norm, which ordinarily have little historical consequence or a negligible scientific significance, can be converted into causally important factors. They become determinative to the extent that they are reduplicated. In the further course of development, the previously unprecedented can become more and more of a causally effective precedent. History would never progress if unique events did not contribute to its making. But novelties acquire weight in the total process of determination only as they forfeit their originality and become recurrent.

This dialectical process can be seen at the dawn of humanity. According to the labor theory of social origins, tool-using and tool-making differentiated man from the beasts. The occasional use of natural objects as tools for some momentary purpose by other anthropoids had no enduring evolutionary consequences and brought about no fundamental changes in their animal mode of existence. The *regular and collective* use and fabrication of tools and the habitual skills associated with them converted our primate progenitors into human beings.

The same is true of that sound-tool, language. Sporadic cries of other species had no social significance and made no essential difference in their relations. The reiteration of verbal utterances by our ancestors, in conjunction with their cooperation in labor, created speech. Language is rooted in the reproduction of words, the conventionalization of meaningful references to things, the stabilization of grammatical elements and structures to which Professor Popper has to conform in order to communicate with us.

The main task of historical and social science, according to Marxism, is to find out the pattern of all those regularities and formulate them into laws that express the necessary connections of objective realities in their evolution. Such regularities are not confined to established social structures. They also operate within the evolutionary and revolutionary changes which bring new and higher types of social organization into existence. These processes begin with occasional variations from the customary pattern which massively recur until they acquire power enough to overthrow and replace the old order.

Professor Popper avers, in defiance of the facts, that only variables and not constants shape history. Actually, history is made by the interplay of its constant and variable elements. In its course of development, constants turn into variables and variables into constants—and they do so, not in an arbitrary manner, but in lawful, materially determined ways.

Let us review a case from the history of politics, the relations between monarchy and democracy. In the earlier stages of civilization the sacred monarchy was the predominant form of sovereignty from Egypt to China. For several thousands of years states rose and fell and dynasties came and went while kingship persisted as the rule. Democracy was unknown in Mesopotamian civilization. This remarkable uniformity in the political constitution of the ancient empires was rooted in the essential stability of the economic and social substructures of these agricultural despotisms.

Political democracy first emerged in Greece in the seventh century B.C. as a result of profound changes in the economic conditions and class relations of its most progressive commercial city-states. But this novel kind of government was exceptional, unstable, and short-lived, enduring here and there for little more than two centuries. Kingship in one form or another remained the normal form of the state through all the subsequent stages of class rule, until the more thoroughgoing bourgeois revolutions deposed the monarchies and set up democratic republics in their stead. Even so, parliamentary democracy did not become widespread or deep-seated until the peak of capitalist expansion and stability was reached in the nineteenth century and then was largely restricted to the richest, most favored nations of the West.

The monarchy that monopolized political life at the dawn of class rule has in its twilight become a rarity, a curious decorative relic, because the fundamental historical conditions for its survival and revival are no longer at hand. Popular sovereignty, on the other hand, which was absent in the first civilizations, is today regarded as the normal and most desirable form of government to which even antidemocratic regimes pay lip service. What was once constant has become variable and vanishing; what was nonexistent is on the rise and constantly growing.

The second case, taken from technology, deals with an analogous transformation in the relations between the two major consecutive types of means of labor. Until two hundred years ago men used nothing but hand-tools in production; machines were an insignificant exception. This historical constant was set aside by the large-scale introduction of machinery, an innovation which came about lawfully and comprehensibly by transferring the function of handling the working tool from a human being to a mechanism. The more complex and efficient means of production displaced the more primitive and less productive implements as the capitalists recognized their greater profitability. In factory industry the use of hand-tools is exceptional while machine production is its basis; their roles have become reversed.

This fundamental change in technology generated a host of others which together constitute industrial capitalism. Under this system tens of millions of people get up five to six days a week and go to work for eight hours or more for wages in enterprises operated by capitalist owners for their private profit. Whatever their individual differences and personal preferences, the wage-workers must submit to this standard type of labor relation in order to get their daily bread, pay the landlord monthly, and meet installment loans regularly. This is not an accident but a necessity of capitalism, its fundamental law, the source of its exploitation.

Professor Popper denies that there are any such essential necessities in economic activities and social relations or that the aim of sociology is to discover and explain them in order to foresee their development. He even contends that social systems or "wholes" do not exist as "empirical objects"; they are only "ideal objects." What really exist are "individuals and their actions and reactions," which presumably never acquire a definitely organized or systematized character.

He therefore assigns an entirely different task to the social sciences. Their main task, he tells us, "is to trace the unintended social repercussions of intentional human actions." That is to say, sociology must revolve around an explanation of the accidents rather than the necessities of history.

This is a legitimate subject of social science, although it is not central to it. Sociology should be more concerned with demonstrating the interplay of accident and necessity in history and the conversion of the one into the other as it develops. Nevertheless, the discrepancies between the conscious purposes of human beings and the real results of their activities, which Hegel called "the cunning of reason," that is to say, the irony of history, does pose an important problem for social science.

In order to clarify why this anomaly has been such a pronounced and persistent trait of human affairs to date, it is essential to find out the social and historical circumstances that have prevented the outcome of men's collective activities from coinciding with their avowed aims or will. Professor Popper apparently believes that this is an eternal law and irremediable flaw of history. Actually, this prime feature of past and present history originated in the exchange of commodities and man's consequent loss of control over his social relations issuing from the expansion of exchange relations. This lack of control is most accentuated in the capitalist phase of commodity production. The phenomenon so overwhelms Professor Popper because capitalism is an inherently anarchic system, beyond regulation by its most powerful agencies and privileged beneficiaries.

The conflicting private interests of its constituent parts make it impossible for the plans of an individual, a corporation, or a state to be assured of realization. The main objective of the socialist movement is to do away with the economic sources of this social disorder and establish the material preconditions for bringing man's aims into consonance with his results by eliminating the private ownership of the means of production and planning economic development.

This is abhorrent to Professor Popper, who is a partisan of individualism and free enterprise. The last sentence of his liberal polemic against Marxism reads: "The fight against avoidable misery should be a recognized aim of public policy, while the increase of happiness should be left, in the main, to private initiative."

The theoretical justification for his program is that social science in general, and Marxism in particular, possesses no predictive power that could contribute to effective social control over the next stage of human progress. He would have us believe that our contemporaries, who have proved capable of the intricate computations and constructions required to send spacecraft and their instruments to the moon and to Mars, are unable to discern the forces at work around them on earth and figure out the main lines of their evolution. Or, having analyzed and ascertained these trends, they cannot act consciously and collectively to realize the best alternative.

Fortunately, even pre-Marxist revolutionaries have not been as myopic as the positivist scholar. They have grasped historical necessities before these became actualities. Indeed, a clear and conscious recognition of these was a prerequisite for their realization. In the Declaration of Independence the colonial patriots proclaimed that it was imperative to break loose from English crown rule at least seven years before they succeeded in doing so. Sam Adams saw its urgency much sooner. The Abolitionists understood the necessity for eradicating the institution of slavery as the biggest block to national progress decades before that was done through the Civil War.

Professor Popper maintains, however, that history has no discernible progressive direction. To assume, as historicists and Marxists do, that we can know where a social structure is—or is not—heading is to arrogate a divine foresight forbidden mere mortals. According to his highly subjective and idealist conception, history can have only the meaning individuals ascribe to it.

This is contradicted by the entire march of history. Every primitive people and outlived ruling class expected to perpetuate themselves and projected that wish upon their historical horizons. In North America the Indians, the feudalists, and the slaveholders asserted their will to survival through furious resistance. Yet all were swept under by the invincible forces of bourgeois civilization. Their subjective desires could not prevail over historical necessities.

Why, then, should scientific socialism be prohibited

from analyzing the structure and functioning of capitalism, identifying the strategic forces and factors which affect its development, foreseeing their further trends (at least in outline if not in concrete detail), and devising a practical program of revolutionary action? Is there any empirical evidence that this can be done? The *Communist Manifesto* of 1848 was so prescient that even today it is more pertinent to contemporary realities than any other political document of its time.

Here are two other examples of Marxist foresight, one confirmed in a positive, the other in a negative manner. In 1906 Trotsky set forth his theory of the permanent revolution, which predicted that the proletariat would have to take power and adopt socialist measures in the coming Russian revolution. That is what happened in 1917.

Twelve years later the exiled Russian Marxist declared in a series of writings that German capitalism had been plunged into so severe a crisis by the crash of 1929 that the shaky Weimar Republic was doomed. The crisis could be resolved only by victory for the socialist working class or by its defeat at the hands of the fascists. He warned that the mistaken policies of the Social-Democratic and Communist leaderships were preparing a catastrophe and forecast that Nazism in power would crush the entire German labor movement, destroy democracy, unleash world war, and attack the Soviet Union. Although his alarms went unheeded, their correctness was substantiated by the events of the next fifteen years.

This example is pertinent to another one of Professor Popper's strictures. The conclusions of the historicists are unfounded and unverifiable prophecies rather than scientific predictions, he contends, because they are unconditional. However, Marxist prognoses, which should flow from an all-sided diagnosis of the given situation, are not presented with such absoluteness. Where there are opposing necessities at work, the outcome must be conditional on their further interaction and relative weight.

Proceeding from a knowledge of the laws of the class struggle and their specific refraction in the Germany of the Weimar Republic, Trotsky concluded that the rickety bourgeois democracy could not be saved and only two opposing roads were open under the given circumstances: fascism or socialism. He stated that all the objective conditions for another October 1917 were present but that the subjective factors of correct leadership would have to be brought to bear for the favorable variant to be achieved. If the divided leadership of the working masses failed to apply the right policies in time, Hitler would win. The perspectives which guided his recommendations for action were conditional, although the possible outcomes were categorical.

The same conditionality applies to judgments on the prospects of the conflict between capitalism and socialism on a world historical scale. The triumph of the socialist cause is not predetermined in the same way as an astronomical eclipse, since the factor of human consciousness and timely action is involved and is decisive. If a cosmic catastrophe or a nuclear war should blow up the planet, that would end human history and dispose, among other things, of the controversy between positivism and Marxism.

Assuming, however, as one must, that mankind will have a future and a better one, victory for the international working class depends upon many factors: the course of development and degree of disintegration of monopoly capitalism, the growth in power of the workers' states, the advances of the colonial revolution, the actions and consciousness of the industrial workers in the imperialist strongholds, the kind of political organization and leadership they get.

It is possible for all the conditions required for a successful socialist revolution to be met. The overthrow of capitalism is no longer the wholly conditional or conjectural prospect it was when Marx and Engels predicted its advent in the *Communist Manifesto*. It is already an accomplished fact in countries on three continents.

As an empiricist, Professor Popper would maintain that no amount of precedents establishes a rule. He does not understand that what has been more or less possible becomes more and more probable, and eventually necessary, as the conditions for its occurrence and recurrence pile up and come together. What has hitherto been conditional, at a certain critical turning point in the processes of development, becomes necessary.

His death is conditional and avoidable at any time of his life; it is more and more probable as he ages and inevitable in the long run because of the laws of his biological constitution. Social systems are no more immortal than the human beings whose activities sustain them. Like capitalism, they can perish piecemeal before they are abolished *in toto*.

Let us consider a fresh historical instance which is most favorable to his viewpoint. The Cuban Revolution developed in an unexpected fashion which surprised not only the Cuban property owners and the corporations and government of the United States, but also the July 26th leaders and the entire world socialist movement. Yet, even if it was not specifically predicted before the fact, its line of development can be explained after the fact.

Political analysts should first ask: Why did the Cuban Revolution follow a different path and have an outcome different from its Latin-American predecessors in Mexico, Bolivia, and Guatemala? There were numerous reasons for its unprecedented turn. Among these was the fact that Castro and his associates learned from the military coup in Guatemala in 1954 that, if colonialism was to be stamped out and popular power preserved, the officer corps and the old army had to be destroyed and replaced by a revolutionary armed force. In addition, they learned how to expropriate the capitalists and start building a planned economy from Russia, Yugoslavia, and China. The whole experience of twentieth-century history since 1917, plus the international balance of forces issuing from it, were indispensable preconditions for the unanticipated course taken by the Fidelistas.

The transformation of the armed insurrection against Batista's capitalist dictatorship into a proletarian-peasant revolution is a spectacular example of the law governing the present stage of world history that the fundamental problems of backward countries cannot be solved except by a revolutionary struggle directed along socialist lines. This theorem of the permanent revolution formulates an irrepressible and growing tendency inherent in all the insurgent colonial movements of our time.

The positivist professor must protest against this logic of contemporary history. The Cuban experience, he will expostulate, was unique; it cannot be taken as a sample of a law. "Society is changing, developing. Its development is not, in the main, a repetitive one." Contrary to his shortsighted philosophy, the Cuban Revolution is not regarded as unique either by its leaders or its enemies. Its general import and impact is what makes it such a touchy issue in American and world politics.

Official Washington does not view Cuba as an isolated incident that can have no sequel, although it would like to have it that way. That was demonstrated by its armed intervention in the Dominican Republic in 1965 and declared intention to dispatch troops elsewhere in Latin America if a comparable threat arises. Both sides recognize the potential for further Cubas in the Western hemisphere and are taking appropriate measures to promote or prevent them.

The policies of Washington to contain and crush, and of Havana to aid and extend, the socialist revolution have a lawful character. They correspond to the logic and dynamics of current history, which is determined and directed by the necessities of the mortal combat between capitalism and socialism.

Standing helplessly between the class adversaries, Professor Popper would advise them that no such necessities exist. Since both sides know better, his advice would fall on deaf ears.

Professor Popper is acclaimed in scholarly circles for his special definition of the nature of scientific method. He teaches that the essence of science consists not so much in the verification of hypotheses as in their falsification. The greatest scientific progress is registered when it is disclosed not what theories and laws can tell us about what exists and what can be done, but when they advise us what does not exist and what cannot be done. Laws above all set limits to the possible.

The timidity of his skeptical epistemology is evident in this lopsided conception of scientific lawfulness. To be sure, the clarification of the conditional limits, inadequacies, and errors of existing theories are an indispensable and fruitful function of scientific activity, a prime source of its growth, the starting point for fresh advances and breakthroughs. That happened in the nineteenth and early twentieth centuries with Euclidean geometry, Newtonian physics, and classical political economy.

But exposures of this kind, which have stimulated progressive crises in science, represent only one phase, one step in the totality of scientific investigation and advancement. It is the negative side of the unending process of acquiring more precise and deepgoing understanding of the phenomena in question. Such revisions in the light of further experimental facts pave the way for the elaboration and verification of more comprehensive, complex, and correct theories. Darwin banished incorrect doctrines from biology as part of his positive demonstration of the evolutionary mechanism and unity of living beings. The eventual outcome, the net result, is a steady accumulation of more ample and dependable information with which to foresee and control natural and social processes.

Ironically, positivism shies away from acknowledging this growth of positive knowledge about the world, does not properly assess its significance and its role and relevance in providing foresight and facilitating action. It is incorrectly named and should be more precisely termed "negativism."

Finally, Professor Popper, who insists that the social sciences cannot and should not forecast historical developments and that unconditional laws are taboo, fails to abide by these two precepts of his own position. Despite his contention that the future is opaque, this liberal does not hesitate to affirm most categorically that revolution in general, and above all the socialist revolution heralded by Marxism, is bound to be ruinous. "I am convinced that revolutionary methods can only make things worse—that they will increase unnecessary suffering; that they will lead to more and more violence; and that they must destroy freedom."

On what scientific grounds, empirical or rational, can such an unconditional assertion be justified? Many past revolutions have benefited mankind and enlarged freedom for the masses. The very bourgeois democracy he defends and cherishes was the offspring of revolutionary struggles. The American people have had two revolutions which made things much better rather than worse for them. Is it then only contemporary proletarian, and not previous bourgeois, revolutions that are full of evils?

He will not convince the peoples of the Soviet Union, Yugoslavia, China, and Cuba that their revolutions brought no good, whatever their shortcomings. Nor will his timid admonitions prevent other peoples from seeking and finding the revolutionary socialist method of solving their otherwise insoluble problems.

This empiricist turns rigidly dogmatic when he confronts the prospect of socialist revolution. In order to uphold gradualism and piecemeal reform at all costs, he is compelled to throw overboard the principles of his own method and relapse into "ahistoricism," an absolute rule that revolutions always and everywhere have baneful results.

Such inconsistency is a congenital vice of positivist epistemology. It is engendered in the last analysis by the predicament of the middle-class liberal under monopoly capitalism who wishes to work toward a better society but fears to overstep the framework of the established order in his views, perspectives, and actions. Others, who refuse to be hemmed in by these arbitrary and essentially reactionary standards, are told that they are "unscientific." This demonstrates how different conceptions of science and its methods, which appear so remote and detached from everyday life, have their social implications, class affiliations, and political uses.

Professor Popper's views have been worth presenting and refuting at length because they are so representative of current empiricism and tellingly reveal the class content and political relevance of rival philosophical positions and conceptions of scientific and logical method. Modern university scholastics teach that philosophy and logic can be—and ought to be—kept apart from social questions and political struggles. But when theory and practice, science and social activity are so divorced, they are rendered barren and devitalized. They need to be mated to be most productive.

Moreover, it is really impossible to cut the one off from the other. The most formally aloof philosophy has specific historical causes, class affiliations, social and political consequences. The most mindless sort of activity has a rationale and method buried within it which analysis can bring to light.

Every great social movement creates, selects, adapts, and applies a set of general ideas and a world outlook that conforms to the situation and interests of its participants and best promotes their needs, activities, and objectives. It is quite logical that empiricism and positivism are the favored modes of thought of liberalism and reformism while dialectical materialism is the appropriate method of scientific socialism. The one is the method of theoretical confusion and practical irresolution; the other of clarity and consistent revolutionary practice.

The forces and tendencies pressed between the polar classes in modern society resort to some sort of philosophy that justifies conciliation, vacillation, opposition to extremes, half-measures. Those who are not sure where they really stand, where they are going or ought to go, or what historical alternatives they actually face, feel at home with the superficial and short-range viewpoint fostered by empiricism. The representatives of uncompromising resistance to monopolist domination and imperialist reaction and the preparers of its overthrow look for a consistent, thoroughgoing, verifiable analysis of natural and social reality which can help them pursue and fulfill their aims.

In summation

The preceding pages have endeavored to show that empiricism is disqualified as a truly scientific philosophy because it does not take definite and correct positions on a series of fundamental theoretical issues.

1) It is unclear and uncertain on the reality and primacy of the objective world independent of man and his apprehension of it.

2) It does not recognize the essential dialectical mobility, interconnections, interactions, and mutual convertibility of all things.

3) It doubts the possibility of attaining true knowledge of reality and has no firm criteria for defining the basis of truth and error and discriminating one from the other.

4) It denies the existence of determinism, causal relations, and lawfulness in nature, society, and thought, thereby removing the ground from scientific objectivity and the most rational activity.

5) It distorts the meaning, content, and value of science as genuine information about the objective material world and as the surest means of mastering its processes for social ends.

6) It disjoins theory from practice, falsifying their actual interdependence in a way that cripples both sides of human endeavor.

Once a progressive and even revolutionary doctrine, the numerous progeny of empiricism now exert a retrograde influence. Empirical theories retain the greatest power and popularity where capitalism is strongest and its organized opposition weakest.

There is an obvious conclusion to be drawn from the significant connection between these facts. The forces dedicated to a better social order can gain strength and understanding by discarding outworn and defective empirical habits of thought. Only the philosophy of Marxism, which stands at the apex of sociological and scientific development, can assure the finding of satisfactory answers to the most complex and compelling issues of this age of transition from capitalism to socialism.

SELECTED SECONDARY SOURCES IN ENGLISH FOR READING AND REFERENCE

Aaron, R.I., *John Locke.* Oxford, 1955.

Anderson, J., *Studies in Empirical Philosophy.* Sydney, 1962.

Attlee, C.R., *As It Happened.* London, 1954.

Ayer, A.J., *British Empirical Philosophers.* London, 1952.

———*The Foundations of Empirical Knowledge.* London, 1940.

———*Language, Truth and Logic.* New York, 1950.

———ed., *Logical Positivism:* An Anthology. Glencoe, 1959

Basson, H.H., *David Hume.* Penguin Books, 1958.

Broad, C.D., *Berkeley's Argument About Material Substance.* London, 1942.

Copleston, S.J., *A History of Philosophy,* vol. V, Hobbes to Hume. London, 1959.

Cornforth, M., *Marxism and the Linguistic Philosophy.* New York, 1965.

———*The Open Philosophy and the Open Society.* New York, 1968.

———*Science Versus Idealism.* London, 1955.

Crowther, J.G., *Francis Bacon.* London, 1960.

De Santillana, G. & Zilsel, E., *The Development of Rationalism and Empiricism.* International Encyclopedia of Unified Science, vol. II, No. 8. Chicago, 1941.

Dunham, B., *Thinkers and Treasurers.* New York, 1960.

Engels, F., *On Historical Materialism.* Karl Marx: Selected Works, vol. 1. New York, 1936.

Farrington, B., *Francis Bacon, Philosopher of Industrial Science.* New York, 1949.

Gardiner, Patrick, ed., *Theories of History.* Glencoe, 1955.

Gibson, J., *Locke's Theory of Knowledge and Its Historical Relations.* Cambridge, 1931.

Hicks, G.D., *Berkeley.* London, 1932.

Huxley, T., *David Hume.* London, 1879.

Johnston, G.A., *The Development of Berkeley's Philosophy.* New York, 1965.

Kolakowski, Leszek, *The Alienation of Reason.* New York, 1968.

Lenin, V.I., *Materialism and Empirio-Criticism.* New York, 1936.

Macpherson, C.B., *The Political Theory of Possessive Individualism.* Oxford, 1962.

Martin, C.B. & Armstrong, D.M., eds., *Locke and Berkeley.* New York, 1968.
Martineau, J., *Essays,* vol. III. London, 1890–91.
Morris, C.R., *Locke, Berkeley, Hume.* Oxford, 1931.
Muirhead, J.H., ed., *Contemporary British Philosophy:* Third Series. London, 1956.
O'Connor, D.J., *John Locke.* Penguin Books, 1952.
Seth, J., *English Philosophers and Schools of Philosophy.* New York, 1925.
Stephen, L., *History of English Thought in the Eighteenth Century.* London, 1876.
Trotsky, L., *In Defense of Marxism.* New York, 1942.
Warnock, G.J., *Berkeley.* Penguin Books, 1953.
Wild, J.D., *George Berkeley.* Cambridge, 1936.
Willey, B., *The Seventeenth Century Background.* London, 1946.
Yolton, J.W., *John Locke and the Way of Ideas.* Oxford, 1956.

INDEX

WORKS BY GEORGE NOVACK

Democracy and Revolution

The limitations and advances of various forms of democracy in class society, from its roots in ancient Greece through its rise and decline under capitalism. Discusses the emergence of Bonapartism, military dictatorship, and fascism, and how democracy will be advanced under a workers and farmers regime. $17

The Origins of Materialism

The rise of a scientific world outlook in ancient Greece, and the development of agriculture, manufacturing, and trade that prepared the way for it. $15

America's Revolutionary Heritage

Marxist Essays

A materialist explanation of the American Revolution, Civil War and Radical Reconstruction, genocide against the Indians, rise of American imperialism, first wave of the fight for women's rights, and more. $23

Polemics in Marxist Philosophy

Novack defends scientific socialism, answering those who, parading as the true interpreters of Marx, have provided a "philosophical" veneer for the anti-working-class political course of Stalinist and social democratic misleaderships around the world. $20

An Introduction to the Logic of Marxism

Marxism is dialectical, Novack explains. It considers all phenomena in their development, in their transition from one state to another. And it is materialist, explaining the world as matter in motion that exists prior to and independently of human consciousness. $12. Also in Farsi.

'THE HISTORY OF EXISTING SOCIETY IS THE HISTORY OF CLASS STRUGGLES'

Labor, Nature, and the Evolution of Humanity

The Long View of History

FREDERICK ENGELS
KARL MARX, GEORGE NOVACK
MARY-ALICE WATERS

Without understanding that social labor, transforming nature, has driven humanity's evolution for millions of years, working people are unable to see beyond the capitalist epoch of class exploitation that warps all human relations, ideas, and values. $12. Also in Spanish and French.

Woman's Evolution

From Matriarchal Clan to Patriarchal Family

EVELYN REED

An expedition from prehistory to class society that reveals women's contributions to civilization and pinpoints the historical factors that led to the subordination of women as a sex. Reed offers new insights on the struggle against women's oppression and for the liberation of humanity. $25. Also in Spanish, Farsi, Indonesian.

The Origin of the Family, Private Property, and the State

FREDERICK ENGELS

The emergence of class-divided society gave rise to repressive state bodies and the oppression of women to enable the ruling classes to pass along wealth and privilege. Engels discusses the consequences for working people of these class institutions—from their ancient forms to their modern versions. $15. Also in Spanish and Farsi.

The Communist Manifesto

KARL MARX
AND FREDERICK ENGELS

Communism, say the founding leaders of the revolutionary workers movement, is not a set of ideas or preconceived "principles" but workers' line of march to power. It springs from a "movement going on under our very eyes." $5. Also in Spanish, French, Farsi, Arabic.

Understanding History

Marxist Essays

GEORGE NOVACK

How did capitalism arise? Why and when did this exploitative system exhaust its once revolutionary role? Why is revolutionary change fundamental to human progress? $15

Capital

KARL MARX

Marx explains the workings of the capitalist system and how it produces the insoluble contradictions that breed class struggle. He demonstrates the inevitability of the revolutionary transformation of society into one ruled for the first time by the producing majority, the working class. Three volumes, $18 each. Also in Spanish. Volume 1 available in French.

Sexism and Science

EVELYN REED

Are human beings innately aggressive? Does biology condemn women to remain the "second sex"? Taking up such biases cloaked as the findings of science, Reed explains that the disciplines closest to human life—anthropology, biology, and sociology—are permeated with rationalizations for the oppression of women and the maintenance of the established capitalist order. $15. Also in Farsi and Arabic.

THE WORKING CLASS AND THE FIGHT AGAINST JEW-HATRED

The Fight Against Jew-Hatred and Pogroms in the Imperialist Epoch

Stakes for the International Working Class

V.I. LENIN, LEON TROTSKY
FARRELL DOBBS, JAMES P. CANNON
JACK BARNES, DAVE PRINCE

Jew-hatred and pogroms—such as Hamas carried out on October 7, 2023—are part of the social convulsions and wars of the imperialist epoch. The authors explain why fighting Jew-hatred is decisive to the working class and oppressed nations of the world—and *what is to be done to end it*. $10. Also in Spanish, French, Greek.

Imperialism's March Toward Fascism and War

JACK BARNES

"There will be new Hitlers, new Mussolinis. That is inevitable. What is not inevitable is that they will triumph. The working-class vanguard will organize our class to fight back against the devastating toll we are made to pay for the capitalist crisis. The future of humanity will be decided in the contest between these contending class forces." In *New International* no. 10. $14. Also in Spanish, French, Farsi, Greek.

The Jewish Question

A Marxist Interpretation

ABRAM LEON

The battle against reactionary forces aiming to exterminate the Jews remains central to world politics, as shown by the genocidal October 2023 pogrom in Israel. Why is Jew-hatred still raising its ugly head? What are its class roots? Why, as Abram Leon explains, is there no solution "independent of the world proletarian revolution"? Revised translation, new introduction, 40 pages of illustrations and maps. $17. Also in Spanish, French, Greek.

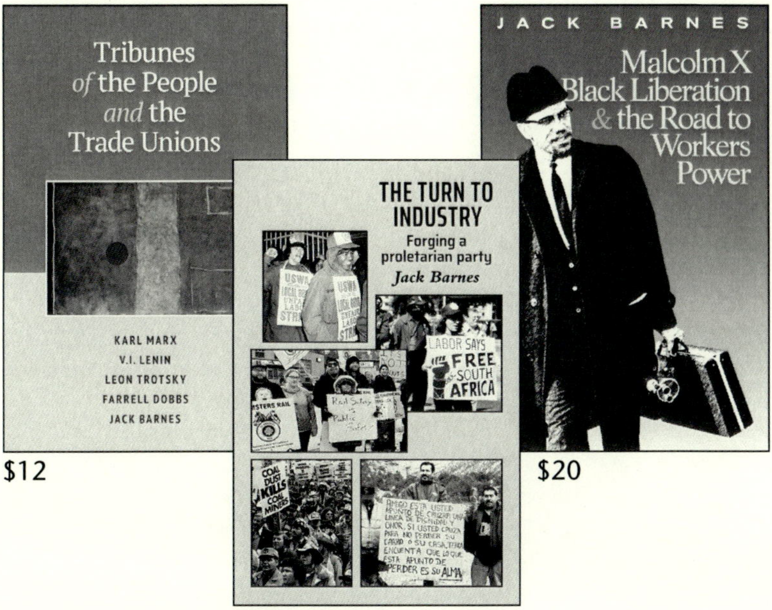

$12

$15

$20

Three books to be read as one . . .

about building a party that's working class in program, composition, and action. One that recognizes, in word and deed, the most revolutionary fact of our time . . .

. . . that working people have the power to create a different world as we act together to defend our own class interests—not those of the privileged classes who exploit our labor, not of those who fear us as "deplorables," or just plain "trash."

As we advance along a revolutionary course toward workers power, we will transform ourselves and awaken to our own worth. Also in Spanish, French, Farsi, Greek.

Special Offer!
All three $30

The Turn to Industry and *Tribunes of the People and the Trade Unions* $20

Either book plus *Malcolm X, Black Liberation, and the Road to Workers Power* $25

PATHFINDERPRESS.COM

CAPITALIST CRISIS AND THE FIGHT FOR WORKERS POWER

The Low Point of Labor Resistance Is Behind Us

The Socialist Workers Party Looks Forward

JACK BARNES, MARY-ALICE WATERS
STEVE CLARK

The global order imposed by Washington is shattering. A long retreat by the working class and unions has come to an end. The bosses and their government are stepping up attacks on our wages, conditions, and constitutional rights. This book highlights opportunities for building a mass proletarian party able to lead the struggle to end capitalist rule, opening a socialist future for humanity. $10. Also in Spanish, French, Greek.

Are They Rich Because They're Smart?

Class, Privilege, and Learning Under Capitalism

JACK BARNES

Exposes growing class inequalities in the US and the self-serving rationalizations of well-paid professionals who think their "brilliance" equips them to "regulate" working people, who don't know what's in our own best interest. $10. Also in Spanish, French, Farsi, Arabic, Greek.

Teamster Rebellion

FARRELL DOBBS

The 1934 strikes that won union recognition for truckers and warehouse workers in Minneapolis and helped pave the way for the working-class social movement that built the industrial unions. The first of four volumes by a central leader of these battles and of the Socialist Workers Party. $16. Also in Spanish, French, Farsi, Greek.

New International

A MAGAZINE OF MARXIST POLITICS AND THEORY

NEW INTERNATIONAL NO. 7

Opening Guns of World War III: Washington's Assault on Iraq

JACK BARNES

The murderous assault on Iraq in 1990–91 heralded increasingly sharp conflicts among imperialist powers, growing instability of capitalism, and more wars. Also includes:

1945: When US Troops Said 'No!'
by Mary-Alice Waters

Lessons from the Iran-Iraq War
by Samad Sharif
$14. Also in Spanish, French, Farsi.

NEW INTERNATIONAL NO. 11

U.S. Imperialism Has Lost the Cold War

JACK BARNES

The collapse of regimes across Eastern Europe and the USSR claiming to be communist did not mean workers and farmers there had been crushed. In today's sharpening class conflicts and wars, these toilers are joining working people the world over in the class struggle against capitalist exploitation. $14. Also in Spanish, French, Farsi, Greek.

NEW INTERNATIONAL NO. 12

Capitalism's Long Hot Winter Has Begun

JACK BARNES

Today's global capitalist crisis is but the opening stage of decades of economic, financial, and social convulsions and class battles. Class-conscious workers confront this historic turning point for imperialism with confidence, Jack Barnes writes, drawing satisfaction from being "in their face" as we chart a revolutionary course to take power. $14. Also in Spanish, French, Farsi, Arabic, Greek.

CUBA'S SOCIALIST REVOLUTION AND THE WORLD

New!

Revolution and the Road to Peace in Colombia

The Example of the Cuban Revolution

FIDEL CASTRO

"No crime can be committed in the name of revolution," Fidel Castro declares, drawing from the example set by working people of Cuba as they took state power out of the hands of its capitalist rulers. In 2008, as part of efforts to end six decades of armed conflict in Colombia, he shared the exemplary record of Cuba's revolutionary struggle with the Revolutionary Armed Forces of Colombia (FARC) and the world. $10. Also in Spanish.

Cuba and the Coming American Revolution

JACK BARNES

This is a book about the example set by the Cuban people that socialist revolution is not only necessary—it can be made. A book about the struggles of workers and other exploited producers in the imperialist heartland, and the youth attracted to them. About the class struggle in the US, where the revolutionary capacities of working people are as utterly discounted by the ruling powers as were those of the Cuban toilers. $10. Also in Spanish, French, Farsi.

'Cuba Will Never Adopt Capitalist Methods'

FIDEL CASTRO

Cuba's rectification process, its contributions to building socialism worldwide, and the victory of Cuban-Angolan-SWAPO forces against the South African army in southern Angola in early 1988. $5

EXPAND YOUR REVOLUTIONARY LIBRARY

Che Guevara on Economics and Politics in the Transition to Socialism

CARLOS TABLADA

It's essential for working people to win state power, said Ernesto Che Guevara. "Then there's the second stage, maybe more difficult than the first"—the transition from dog-eat-dog capitalism to socialism. Includes Fidel Castro's 1987 speech "Che's Ideas Are Absolutely Relevant Today." New edition with substantially expanded selections from Guevara's writings. $17. Also in Spanish.

Thomas Sankara Speaks

The Burkina Faso Revolution, 1983–87

Under Sankara's guidance, Burkina Faso's revolutionary government led peasants, workers, women, and youth to expand literacy; to sink wells, plant trees, erect housing; to combat women's oppression; to carry out land reform; to join others worldwide to free themselves from the imperialist yoke. $20. Also in French.

In Defense of Marxism

Against the Petty-Bourgeois Opposition in the Socialist Workers Party

LEON TROTSKY

A reply to those in the revolutionary workers movement in the late 1930s who buckled to bourgeois patriotism during Washington's buildup to enter World War II. Trotsky explains why only a party fighting to bring workers into its ranks and leadership can steer a communist course. In the process, he defends the materialist and dialectical foundations of Marxism. $17. Also in Spanish, French, Farsi.

Lenin's Final Fight

Speeches and Writings, 1922–23

V.I. LENIN

In 1922 and 1923, V.I. Lenin, central leader of the world's first socialist revolution, waged what was to be his last political battle—one that was lost after his death. At stake was whether that revolutionary government and the world communist movement it led would remain on the revolutionary proletarian course that brought workers and peasants to power in Russia in 1917. $17. Also in Spanish, Farsi, Greek.

Malcolm X Talks to Young People

"The young generation of whites, Blacks, browns, whatever else—you're living at a time of revolution," said Malcolm in 1964. "And I for one will join with anyone, I don't care what color you are, as long as you want to change this miserable condition that exists on this earth." Four talks and an interview in the last months of Malcolm's life. $12. Also in Spanish, French, Farsi, Greek.

Pathfinder Press **accessible e-books** for the blind, those with low vision, or other challenges reading print books

For a list of current accessible titles, go to: pathfinderpress.com/collections/books-for-the-blind.

Visit bookshare.org for information on how to sign up.

PATHFINDERPRESS.COM